THE
SUPER EASY
5-INGREDIENT
COOKBOOK

THE SUPER EASY
5-INGREDIENT
COOKBOOK

30-MINUTE | SHEET PAN | ONE POT | NO-COOK RECIPES

SARAH WALKER CARON

ROCKRIDGE
PRESS

Interior designer: KPhD
Cover designer: Katy Brown
Production Editor: Erum Khan
Cover photography © Hélène Dujardin, Food styling by Lisa Rovick; interior and back cover photography ©Nadine Greeff
Author photo © Gabor Degre, Bangor Daily News

ISBN: Print 978-1-64152-152-9 | eBook 978-1-64152-153-6

For Will and Paige

There's always time to eat well, even when life gets busy.

CONTENTS

Introduction

The sweet aroma of apples simmering with cinnamon; the sizzle of sausage on a griddle; the heat rising from the grill as burgers cook over charcoal—all of these things evoke memories, yearnings, desires.

For me, these are bits of childhood—the woven tapestry of experiences and memories that comprise the happy moments growing up. It's Sunday mornings with my aunt at the stove, holiday breakfasts lovingly arranged by my mother on the trestle table my uncle built, and sitting outside while my grandfather tended the kettle grill. It's all simple, and yet not at all simple.

Food is nourishment. The vitamins, minerals, and nutrients are a puzzle that forms the building blocks of our day. Food fuels our bodies and minds. But it's more than that. I love the adage "Food is love," because it is. Creating food for those you care about is nothing short of an act of love. When you knowingly make a favorite food for a loved one, you are saying, "I see you." That's a powerful message.

Food is also a conversation starter. Around the dinner table, we gather to talk about our day over bowls of pasta and platters of chicken. Over a spread of tacos, we might discuss what's in the news, what we have on our to-do lists, or the books we're reading. Nestled at the table, I hear about what my kids are learning, the sports they play, playground drama, and life concerns.

Food is also ritual. My family has a long-standing tradition of Christmas brunch, served just after the presents are opened but before we all retire to nap, read, and play. Served on brightly colored reindeer plates with chilled glasses of orange juice, it's familiar and loaded with foods each of us loves: bagels and lox with all the fixings, chocolate croissants, eggs with bacon and sausage, fruit salad.

But good food—and food rituals—should not be reserved for special occasions. Good food can be had every day and for every meal we eat. And that good food, created simply, can bring us together, nourish us, and form the fondest memories.

That's what this cookbook is all about.

My name is Sarah Walker Caron, and I am a recipe developer, food writer, newspaper editor, magazine editor, college journalism instructor, and—importantly—mom to two growing tweens. A typical week in our house includes multiple nights of running to practice for my son, dance class, a Girl Scout meeting, and a sports practice and game for my daughter, and so much

more. Sound busy? It is! That's why I prefer to cook simple dishes with short ingredient lists and abbreviated cooking times. That's also why writing this cookbook is important to me.

In *The Super Easy 5-Ingredient Cookbook*, every recipe has five ingredients or fewer and can often be prepared, cooked, and on the table in 30 minutes or less.

The recipes in this book reflect how my own family eats—with accessible, everyday ingredients found in many grocery stores. We often start with fresh veggies and fruits, create dishes from scratch, and do it all in as little hands-on time as possible. We use frozen vegetables, and occasionally canned ones (such as canned tomatoes), when it makes sense to do so. We eat a variety of proteins and have vegetarian meals at least a few nights a week.

We eat well, but we don't spend hours cooking. It's the same food point of view I share on my food blog, Sarah's Cucina Bella (www.sarahscucinabella.com).

I hope you'll dig into this book, try the recipes, learn the techniques, and then adapt them to your own preferences. And I hope you'll love the recipes as much as my family does.

May the good food in these pages bring you and your loved ones together.

1

FANTASTIC MEALS IN A FLASH

Some of the best dishes are the simplest ones: a ripe, just-picked tomato sliced and sprinkled with sea salt; warm pasta tossed with butter, salt, and pepper; tender boiled potatoes mashed with butter, salt, pepper, and milk. These dishes aren't complicated, but they speak to our flavor memory. They are familiar and beloved. They remind us of our families, our child-hoods, our pasts. Good food, like those familiar dishes, doesn't have to be complicated. With streamlined techniques and wholesome ingredients, you can cook fresh, healthy, delicious dishes for every meal of the day. As a working single mother, I understand how challenging it can be to get a good dinner on the table at the end of the day. By the time you and the kids get home, you're tired, hungry, and have so many other things to do first. Fortunately, that doesn't have to stand in the way of a nutritious meal. Making good food doesn't have to be time-consuming or taxing. In fact, it can be very quick and easy. Five-ingredient recipes will help. Every recipe in this book is accessible, made with foods you can probably find in your local supermarket. The short ingredient lists mean it won't take long to prepare the dishes. The cooking methods are designed to be easy, too—either fast, hands-off, or able to be prepped ahead of time. The purpose of this book is to make enjoying good food for every meal a simple affair.

The recipes you will find here primarily call for whole foods, meaning the ingredients are often in their purest form—as close to how they grew in nature as possible. You won't find canned soups or boxed mixes in the ingredients lists. You will find natural flavor boosters, like soy sauce and various types of vinegar. I've chosen these for what they add to a recipe and dish—their flavors will never overpower or hide the main ingredients.

This book covers all the basics you need to know to start cooking easy, flavorful meals at home today. Grab some sticky notes or tabs (my favorite for marking pages with recipes I want to try), and dig in.

Ready to get started?

Three Keys to Easy Cooking

Can cooking really be easy? Yes. Without a doubt. Good cooking—the kind that yields well-seasoned, flavorful food—is about using flavors and techniques together to create dishes you and your family will want to eat again and again.

There are three keys you need to get started.

STOCK THE BASICS

A well-stocked pantry and refrigerator are the secret to eating well. When you have basic ingredients on hand, you can easily toss together meals—whether it's a quick breakfast or a last-minute dinner after a long, hard day.

With only basic pantry items, you can make several of the recipes in this book, like the Easy Tomato Marinara (page 143) and the Blueberry Muffin Mug Cake (page 20). However, the other recipes here won't send you on multiple trips all over town to a variety of grocery stores either. Many of the recipes can be made with basic groceries that are easy to find and easy to store.

KEEP IT SIMPLE

Have you read the book *Julie & Julia* by Julie Powell? Powell is a blogger who decided—in a moment of crisis—to cook her way through the entire *Mastering the Art of French Cooking* by Julia Child and blog about it. It's great fun to read, though her stress as she approaches the complicated recipes is palpable.

While complicated recipes have their place and can create amazing foods, you don't need to master the complicated techniques of the culinary arts to have a good meal. This book will help you keep it simple. I want you to use as few dishes, pots, and pans as possible when cooking, while getting wows from everyone who tries your food.

COOK WITH EFFICIENCY

Perhaps the biggest and best way you can make cooking simple and quick is to be efficient. That means gathering your ingredients before you begin cooking, reading recipes all the way through before you start, so you know what's coming, and prepping everything you need. These things make the difference between a 15-minute meal and one that drags on to almost an hour because you started cooking before you were ready.

Good organization goes beyond the moment of cooking though. It's about anticipating what you may need in the pantry and having it all on hand. It's about planning what's for breakfast, lunch, and dinner before it's time to start cooking. And it's about enlisting help when you need it.

Stock the Basics

There are some things you should have in your pantry, refrigerator, and freezer all the time for you to grab and cook. Stock and you won't have to go to the grocery store just to get a meal on the table.

PANTRY STAPLES

The recipes in this book use four pantry staples again and again. These ingredients (plus water) don't count toward each recipe's five ingredients, but they are absolutely essential for tasty and easy dishes.

Salt

To bring out the flavor in dishes, you will need salt. Use it sparingly, adding more as you like. I use Morton's kosher salt for all the recipes in this book, and that's what I recommend you keep on hand. The brand here is important, because all kosher salts are not created equal. Morton's has a unique texture and grain size that I prefer. To duplicate my cooking efforts, you'll need this salt.

Whatever you do, don't substitute table salt in these recipes, as it may result in too-salty dishes. Table salt has a small, uniform grain size because it is processed, and also is likely to have more additives (which is why I prefer the purer kosher salt in my cooking). Because of its grain size, 1 teaspoon of table salt has more salt than 1 teaspoon of kosher salt.

Pepper

I use ground black pepper in a little tin. It's simple, basic, cheap, and convenient. If you want to step up your pepper game a bit, freshly ground black pepper in a small grinder is even better.

Oil

There are two oils I keep on hand all the time. The first is extra-virgin olive oil, which I use in most cooking. It adds a robust flavor to dishes. The second is vegetable oil, which I use in dishes where I don't want the flavor of the oil to change the flavor of the dish (like the mug cakes). You'll also need nonstick cooking spray.

Vinegar

There are so many types of vinegar. Which ones should you keep on hand? The recipes in this book rely on a few vinegars. First, you'll want a good-quality balsamic vinegar. This works in so many of the dishes. Second is seasoned rice vinegar. It's lighter and makes dishes like Garlic-Ginger Carrots (page 39) come alive. I also like to keep red wine vinegar in my pantry. It's excellent in some marinades and dressings.

BASIC GROCERIES

These are the things you'll find in the supermarket that will keep for quite a while in your kitchen cupboards.

Dried or Bulk Items

- Breadcrumbs: Italian seasoned and panko
- Cinnamon, ground
- Cornstarch

- Dried basil
- Dried oregano
- Dried rosemary
- Dried thyme

- Flour: This book uses self-rising flour in several recipes because it makes quick work of otherwise more complicated baked goods, but all-purpose flour is the most versatile; stocking both will enable you to make everything in this book.
- Garlic powder
- Oats
- Pasta
- Rice and/or quinoa
- Smoked paprika
- Soy sauce
- Sugar: white and light brown

Jarred and Canned Goods

- Canned beans
- Canned seafood: tuna, salmon, or crab
- Canned tomatoes: a selection of diced, crushed, and puréed tomatoes
- Roasted red peppers

FROZEN BASICS

Food is always best fresh, but some things are almost as good—and more convenient—frozen.

- Fruit: such as strawberries and blueberries
- Shrimp
- Vegetables: such as chopped spinach, broccoli, and peas
- Premade piecrust
- Puff pastry

FRESH AND VERSATILE INGREDIENTS

I selected the fresh ingredients in this list because they are easy to find, versatile for many recipes, nutritious, delicious, and relatively affordable. Learning to cook with these ingredients will make cooking at home much easier.

If you don't have fresh on hand, tips in the recipes will offer ways to swap some of these fresh ingredients with their frozen, dried, jarred, or canned counterparts.

Fruits

- Apples and pears
- Berries: such as strawberries, blueberries, and raspberries
- Limes and lemons
- Stone fruit: such as peaches and plums

Vegetables

- Avocados
- Bell peppers
- Carrots
- Lettuce
- Onions: red and yellow
- Potatoes
- Sweet potatoes
- Tomatoes

Proteins

Want to stock up? Fresh meats can be frozen and defrosted before cooking.

- Boneless pork chops
- Chicken breasts
- Chicken drumsticks
- Ground beef
- Precooked sausage
- Salmon
- Turkey cutlets
- White fish, such as cod or flounder

Herbs and Seasonings

- Basil
- Cilantro
- Ginger
- Parsley

Keep It Simple

Much like a home, cooking starts with a good foundation. In this case, that means simple recipes like the ones in this book, wholesome ingredients, and basic cooking gear.

When approaching the recipes in this cookbook, it's important to understand that they provide a foundation to cooking. They offer simple, fuss-free ways to cook good food. Once you've mastered them, be bold and modify the recipes to your tastes and desires. Add more to a recipe, if you want, or swap an ingredient for a different one. It's totally okay to experiment with food, and I encourage you do so (after you've tried the recipe as written at least a couple of times, of course).

Got leftovers? In my house, they seldom last long. They often end up being taken for lunches or transformed into other meals. For instance, fried rice and other grain dishes, paired with an egg over easy, become a satisfying breakfast. Leftover veggies are delightful mixed with pasta or served in wraps. And proteins can be chopped up for salad or nacho toppings the next day. Get creative, and don't feel limited to just reheating leftovers.

Smart Shopping Tips

Go with a plan. Before grocery shopping for the week, sit down with your family calendar and figure out what meals you will be making at home. Then plan meals that fit those days best. For breakfasts, make sure there's fruit on hand, easy options such as oatmeal, and ingredients for make-ahead dishes, like the Make-Ahead Freezer Breakfast Sandwiches (page 24) in chapter 2. For lunches, will you be making sandwiches or packing leftovers, or will you make something to be eaten over several days? For dinners, you'll want to figure out what you're having each night before making your shopping list. And don't forget drinks and snacks.

Cook in season. Some recipes can be made any time of year because, for instance, some frozen fruit works just as well as fresh fruit. But others—like the Watermelon-Lime Smoothie (page 16)—are best made in the summertime when the fruit is cheap and plentiful. Likewise, the recipes with asparagus are best made in the spring.

Don't shop hungry. There is no greater enemy of a successful shopping trip than going while you are hungry. That's when the cookies, chips, cheeses, and more start piling up in the cart. Instead, eat something before you go and stick to the list you made.

Use coupons. There are often coupons in your local newspaper, on your grocery store mobile app, and even online for common staple items like canned tomatoes and pasta. Keep an eye out for them to get additional savings while you shop.

Don't overbuy. Food waste is a huge problem in this country. You can do your part to combat it by buying only what you need. Open stock bulk bins are great for this—you can buy just enough lentils, rice, quinoa, and countless other things for a recipe, saving packaging and money in the process. And yes, I said money—often it's cheaper per pound to buy from the bulk bins.

LAST-MINUTE SUBSTITUTIONS

What happens when you are missing an ingredient? First, don't panic. It happens to every-one. It's what you do next that matters. Here are some common swaps for ingredients that can help you keep cooking. While these modifications will change the dishes slightly, they will still be tasty.

- Milk: Use half-and-half or heavy cream, but mix in a little water to thin it out.
- Lime juice: Use lemon juice.
- Lemon juice: Use lime juice.
- Panko: Use regular seasoned breadcrumbs.
- Seasoned breadcrumbs: Use panko mixed with dried Italian herbs, such as basil, oregano, and thyme, or pulverize stale bread in a food processor and mix with seasonings.
- Parmesan cheese: Any hard cheese can be substituted, including Romano and Asiago.
- Honey: Use an equal amount of brown sugar.
- Olive oil: Use vegetable oil.
- Carrots: Sweet potatoes can be used interchangeably, with minimal impact on the flavor.

BASIC KITCHEN EQUIPMENT

The recipes in this book require only the most basic of kitchen equipment. I've pared this list down to a handful of must-haves, and a few extras that would make things a little easier.

Must have

- Mixing bowl set (small, medium, and large): Different sizes let you mix well. Smaller quantities can be hard to adequately mix in a too-large mixing bowl, and big batches need plenty of room for blending.
- Large cutting board
- Knives: I recommend starting with two knives: a utility knife with a 3½- to 4-inch blade and a chef's knife with an 8-inch blade. These are the two knives I use most in my kitchen. The utility knife is perfect for slicing, boning, and some chopping. The chef's knife is essential for mincing, chopping, dicing, and carving.
- Large nonstick skillet or sauté pan
- Nonstick baking sheet
- Large pot (about 6 quarts)
- Medium saucepan (about 3 quarts)

Meal Planning Basics

Planning your meals for the week is a good way to save time and money. That way, you buy just what you need at the supermarket, and you know what you're making each day. I love meal planning for dinners best, because it's the meal where having a plan makes life so much easier.

SAMPLE DINNER MEAL PLAN

Sunday: Herb-Garlic Turkey Tenderloin (page 100) and Spinach Salad with Roasted Grapes (page 36) with Honey-Balsamic Vinaigrette (page 137) (save the leftovers for later in the week)

Monday: Garlic-Parsley Shrimp (page 79) and green beans with rice (make extra rice for Wednesday)

Tuesday: Easy Steak Tacos (page 107) with Spicy Pineapple Salsa (page 139) (save the leftover salsa)

Wednesday: Vegetable Fried Rice (page 50) with fried eggs

Thursday: Turkey-Veggie Wraps (page 96) with leftover Honey-Balsamic Vinaigrette

Friday: Easy Skillet Burgers (page 105) with Garlic-Parsley Sweet Potato Fries (page 42) (have the leftover Spicy Pineapple Salsa with tortilla chips as an appetizer)

Saturday: Spinach-Artichoke Baked Ravioli (page 62)

TIPS FOR MEAL PLANNING SUCCESS

1. **List the days of the week.** Compare these to your family calendar. On busy nights, plan the easiest meals.

2. **Choose a main dish for each dinner.** You need only one main dish. But you'll want to plan a vegetable side dish or two and a carb to go with it. Sometimes the carb can be as simple as a batch of rice or quinoa.

3. **Keep some parts of the meal *really* simple.** Everything doesn't need to be a recipe. Sometimes a frozen steam-in-the-bag side of green beans is perfect for rounding out a meal.

4. **Go through the recipes.** Take note of what you have on hand. Make a list of anything you need. In some cases you might want to note quantity on your shopping list, to be sure you buy enough (or not too much).

5. **Shop to your list.** When you get to the grocery store, buy everything on the list. Remember, it's all there for a reason.

6. **Freeze proteins that won't be used in a few days.** This will ensure their freshness and prevent spoilage.

- Muffin pan: 12-cup
- Loaf pan
- Square glass baking dish: 8-by-8-inch
- Rectangular glass baking dish: 9-by-13-inch
- Blender
- Whisk
- Wooden cooking and mixing spoons
- Measuring spoons
- Measuring cups
- Pastry brush

Nice to have

- Small nonstick skillet: Smaller recipes are best cooked in a small skillet. This is also great for fried eggs and omelets.
- Santoku knife: This is my very favorite knife for mincing. The top of the blade is curved and the bottom is straight. It's known for being perfectly balanced, making quick work of prep. I use one with a 6-inch blade.
- Bread knife: The serrated edge helps cut bread evenly without compressing it.
- Food processor: If you don't have a food processor, you can use a blender for any of the recipes in this book calling for one.
- Spatula

Cook with Efficiency

Cooking is not just finding a recipe and getting started. The way you prepare and execute in the kitchen matters. For best results, you want to take three important steps.

Review and plan. Once you've decided on a recipe, read it thoroughly, including the headnote, ingredient list, directions, and tips. This will help you learn everything that goes into it before you get started so you aren't surprised by a step or thrown off by a direction while cooking.

Mise en place. French for "everything in its place," this cooking term means having all your ingredients and tools at hand and ready before you begin cooking. Sure, these recipes only have five ingredients, but it's still important to gather them all before you start cooking, and prep anything that needs chopping or cutting. That way, when you actually start cooking, you are ready to roll.

Clean as you go. That nursery school song about cleaning up has a lot of relevance. Toss your trash and put away ingredients as you finish with them. Wipe down your prep space when your prep work is done. And load those bowls and cutting boards into the dishwasher right away. It's so much more efficient, and you'll have an easier time cleaning up after dinner if you've done this while you're cooking.

TIMESAVING TIPS AND TRICKS

Prep ahead. Ingredients like carrots, onions, and peppers can be chopped ahead of time and stored in the refridgerator in airtight containers until you are ready to use them. When you do this work in advance, it makes cooking even faster.

Double it up. Soups and pastas make great lunches, and rice has so many uses. When you're cooking things that work for other meals, and when you're preparing ingredients like rice, consider making a double batch so you'll have extra to eat or cook with later. Bonus: You can also freeze most of the soup recipes in this book and defrost and reheat them later.

Cook recipes with similar ingredients. Recipes like Crispy Panko-Crusted Broccoli (page 37) and Tomato and Feta Crostini (page 32) are great to make at the same time. Why? Because one uses lemon zest while the other uses lemon juice, so you can prep one ingredient and make two recipes with it.

Save the bits and pieces. Juicing a lemon or lime? Toss the rind into a freezer bag. It can be zested from frozen later to be used in another recipe. Got leftover berries? If you aren't going to eat them, freeze those, too. And when the bananas get past their prime, peel them and freeze those as well to use in baked goods, frozen yogurt, milkshakes, and more.

Hit the salad bar. No, seriously. In a pinch, you can buy ingredients there that have already been sliced, chopped, and prepped.

About the Recipes

The recipes in this book all contain five ingredients or fewer (remember, that's not counting salt, pepper, oil, nonstick cooking spray, vinegar, and water). Three-quarters of them can also be made in a single pot, pan, or dish and/or cooked in 30 minutes or less, from the start of prep to putting the dish on the table. Keep an eye out for the following labels to help you choose recipes.

RECIPE LABELS

 30-Minute The recipe can be prepped, cooked, and served in 30 minutes or less.

 No-Cook The recipe does not require any cooking at all.

 One The recipe can be cooked in a single pot, pan, or baking dish, or will include a tip for making it in a slow cooker. For no-cook recipes, it can be made in a single bowl or a blender.

 Freezer-Friendly The recipe can be frozen and reheated. I'll give you storage and reheating instructions for all of these.

Some recipes will also have labels indicating that they are suitable for some special diets (or can be modified to make them so).

 Gluten-Free

 Vegetarian

 Vegan

Most of the recipes will also include a tip on how to modify the dish or substitute ingredients. Look for:

Variation

- Substituting or adding extra ingredients to vary the flavor, texture, or some other aspect of the dish.
- Substituting ingredients to make the dish vegan, vegetarian, or gluten-free. (Remember to always look for gluten-free labels to ensure ingredients like oats were processed in a gluten-free facility.)

Make It Easier

- Substituting frozen, jarred, canned, or dried versions of a fresh ingredient.
- Sharing culinary tips and tricks to prep an ingredient more easily.
- In one-pot recipes, how to make the dish in a slow cooker.

STRAWBERRY-KIWI SMOOTHIE, PAGE 18

SMOOTHIES AND BREAKFASTS

Watermelon-Lime Smoothie

SERVES 4

PREP TIME:
5 MINUTES

30-MINUTE

GF
GLUTEN-FREE

NO-COOK

ONE

VEGETARIAN

One of my fondest childhood memories is eating watermelon at a school picnic, the juices running down my arms and staining my white sneakers. This refreshing smoothie tastes of summer days, cookouts, and picnics on the beach—without the grit, of course. Ready in minutes, it's a great drink to start the day.

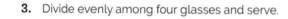

6 cups cubed watermelon
(about ¼ watermelon)

1 cup vanilla Greek yogurt
Juice of 1 lime (about ¼ cup)

1. In a blender, combine the watermelon, yogurt, and lime juice.

2. Blend until smooth.

3. Divide evenly among four glasses and serve.

MAKE IT EASIER: Cut the watermelon ahead of time and store in a covered dish in the refrigerator so you can just dump the ingredients into the blender and purée.

PER SERVING (ABOUT ¾ CUP) CALORIES: 110; TOTAL FAT: 2G; SATURATED FAT: 1G; CHOLESTEROL: 8MG; SODIUM: 31MG, CARBOHYDRATES: 21G; FIBER: 1G; PROTEIN: 4G

Banana Cream Pie Smoothie

Bananas are my son's very favorite fruit, so we always have some in our kitchen. The slightly past ripe ones are best in this recipe. This sweet, creamy smoothie is meant to be sipped along with something else, like toast or fruit salad.

SERVES 4

PREP TIME:
5 MINUTES

30-MINUTE

NO-COOK

ONE

VEGETARIAN

1 cup vanilla Greek yogurt

1 cup milk

4 bananas, peeled and broken into chunks

4 shortbread cookies or 1 full graham cracker

1. In a blender, combine the yogurt, milk, bananas, and cookies.

2. Blend until smooth.

3. Divide evenly among four glasses and serve.

VARIATION: Substitute regular vanilla yogurt for the Greek yogurt. If you do this, the smoothie will be less thick and the flavor may be slightly sweeter. You can also sub in gluten-free cookies or crackers to make this smoothie gluten-free.

PER SERVING (ABOUT ¾ CUP) CALORIES: 186; TOTAL FAT: 5G; SATURATED FAT: 3G; CHOLESTEROL: 14MG; SODIUM: 64MG; CARBOHYDRATES: 34G; FIBER: 3G; PROTEIN: 5G

Strawberry-Kiwi Smoothie

SERVES 4

PREP TIME:
10 MINUTES

30-MINUTE

GF
GLUTEN-FREE

ONE

NO-COOK

VEGETARIAN

When a dear friend tried this smoothie, she proclaimed it to be exactly what a smoothie is meant to be: smooth and fruity. This big portion is a meal all by itself.

3 cups halved strawberries

2 kiwi fruits, peeled

1½ cups vanilla Greek yogurt

1 cup milk

1 tablespoon honey

1. In a blender, combine the strawberries, kiwi, yogurt, milk, and honey.

2. Blend on high until smooth.

3. Divide evenly among four glasses and serve.

MAKE IT EASIER: The best way to peel a kiwi is to halve it and scoop out the flesh with a spoon.

PER SERVING (ABOUT ¾ CUP) CALORIES: 168; TOTAL FAT: 6G; SATURATED FAT: 3G; CHOLESTEROL: 18MG; SODIUM: 69MG; CARBOHYDRATES: 26G; FIBER: 3G; PROTEIN: 6G

Power Green Smoothie

It doesn't take much banana to sweeten and flavor this smoothie, but the apple taste is unmistakable. What you won't taste, though, is the spinach, which adds extra nutrients to this smoothie. I love making this for my son after track practice.

SERVES 4

PREP TIME:
5 MINUTES

(30)
30-MINUTE

GF
GLUTEN-FREE

ONE

NO-COOK

VEGETARIAN

2 green apples, cored and cut into chunks

1 banana, peeled

1 cup baby spinach

1 cup vanilla Greek yogurt

1 cup milk

1. In a blender, combine the apples, banana, spinach, yogurt, and milk.

2. Blend on high until smooth.

3. Divide evenly among four glasses and serve.

PER SERVING (ABOUT ¾ CUP) CALORIES: 149; TOTAL FAT: 4G; SATURATED FAT: 2G; CHOLESTEROL: 14MG; SODIUM: 72MG; CARBOHYDRATES: 26G; FIBER: 3G; PROTEIN: 5G

Blueberry Muffin Mug Cake

SERVES 1

PREP TIME:
5 MINUTES

COOK TIME:
2 MINUTES

Gently sweetened and soft, this breakfast mug cake is dotted with blueberries and ready in less than 10 minutes. You will need either a ramekin or a standard 8-ounce mug for this recipe. Eat it with a spoon, right from the mug.

ONE

VEGETARIAN

30-MINUTE

3 tablespoons all-purpose flour

1 tablespoon brown sugar

¼ teaspoon baking powder

2 tablespoons milk

1 tablespoon vegetable oil

Pinch salt

1 tablespoon blueberries

1. In the ramekin or mug, stir together the flour, brown sugar, baking powder, milk, oil, and salt until well combined and smooth. Stir in the blueberries.

2. Microwave on high for 1 to 1½ minutes, until cooked through, and serve.

VARIATION: Fresh or frozen blueberries will work in this recipe, as will fresh or frozen raspberries or blackberries.

PER SERVING CALORIES: 281; TOTAL FAT: 15G; SATURATED FAT: 1G; CHOLESTEROL: 3MG; SODIUM: 105MG; CARBOHYDRATES: 35G; FIBER: 1G; PROTEIN: 4G

Brown Sugar Oatmeal Mug Cake

Oats are such a good breakfast food. Transform them into something special with this easy recipe for a moist, tender, lightly sweetened breakfast cake that you can make in the microwave in 7 minutes from start to finish. You will need either a ramekin or standard 8-ounce mug for this recipe.

SERVES 1

PREP TIME:
5 MINUTES

COOK TIME:
2 MINUTES

30-MINUTE

ONE

VEGETARIAN

¼ cup rolled oats

2 tablespoons all-purpose flour

1 tablespoon brown sugar

¼ teaspoon baking powder

3 tablespoons milk

1 tablespoon vegetable oil

1. In the ramekin or mug, stir together the oats, flour, brown sugar, baking powder, milk, and oil until well combined and smooth.

2. Microwave on high for 1 to 1½ minutes, until cooked through, and serve.

VARIATION: A dash of cinnamon is a nice addition to this recipe. It gives it a rich, warm flavor.

PER SERVING CALORIES: 407; TOTAL FAT: 18G; SATURATED FAT: 2G; CHOLESTEROL: 4MG; SODIUM: 112MG; CARBOHYDRATES: 54G; FIBER: 5G; PROTEIN: 10G

Blueberry Cider Quick Bread

**MAKES 1 LOAF
(8 SLICES)**

PREP TIME:
10 MINUTES

COOK TIME:
1 HOUR

Tender, light, and dotted with blueberries, this bread is great slathered with butter in the morning. Toast it, if you like, or batter it with egg to make French toast. The flavor of the hard cider you use will change the flavor of this bread. I particularly love making this with a pumpkin cider, which has notes of fall flavors.

ONE

VEGAN

Nonstick cooking spray

2⅔ cups self-rising flour

¼ cup light brown sugar

1 (12-ounce) can hard cider

1 cup blueberries

1. Preheat the oven to 375°F. Grease a loaf pan with nonstick cooking spray.

2. In a large mixing bowl, stir together the flour and brown sugar. Stir in the hard cider until fully combined. Stir in the blueberries.

3. Pour the batter into the prepared loaf pan. Tap gently to even it out.

4. Bake for 50 to 60 minutes, until a knife inserted into the loaf comes out clean.

5. Let cool, then turn the bread out onto a platter, slice, and serve.

VARIATION: Don't want to use hard cider? Substitute club soda and add 1 teaspoon each of vanilla extract and ground cinnamon to the recipe.

PER SERVING (1 SLICE) CALORIES: 194; TOTAL FAT: 1G; SATURATED FAT: 0G; CHOLESTEROL: 0MG; SODIUM: 531MG; CARBOHYDRATES: 43G; FIBER: 2G; PROTEIN: 4G

Easy Puff Pastry Orange Sweet Rolls

These flaky rolls are such a treat in the morning. With an infusion of orange inside and in the delightful glaze, it's a nice flavorful change from standard cinnamon rolls.

SERVES 4

PREP TIME:
10 MINUTES

COOK TIME:
30 MINUTES

ONE

VEGETARIAN

1 tablespoon unsalted butter, melted, plus more for brushing

1 sheet frozen puff pastry, defrosted

2 tablespoons brown sugar

Zest of 1 orange

½ cup powdered (confectioners') sugar

2 to 3 teaspoons freshly squeezed orange juice

1. Preheat the oven to 425°F. Brush the inside and bottom of an 8-by-8-inch glass baking dish with some melted butter.

2. Spread the puff pastry out on a cutting board, and brush with the melted butter. Sprinkle all over with brown sugar and orange zest, distributing it evenly over the dough.

3. Roll the dough up into a tube, starting at the long edge. Slice into six pieces, each about 1 inch wide. Place in the prepared baking dish.

4. Bake for 25 to 30 minutes, until golden and cooked through.

5. In a small mixing bowl, stir together the powdered sugar and orange juice. Pour over the sweet rolls and enjoy immediately.

MAKE IT EASIER: If the puff pastry gets very soft, dust the cutting board with a little flour before laying it out, to prevent sticking.

PER SERVING (1½ ROLLS) CALORIES: 430; TOTAL FAT: 24G; SATURATED FAT: 7G; CHOLESTEROL: 8MG; SODIUM: 163MG; CARBOHYDRATES: 49G; FIBER: 1G; PROTEIN: 4G

Make-Ahead Freezer Breakfast Sandwiches

**MAKES
6 SANDWICHES**

PREP TIME:
15 MINUTES

COOK TIME:
30 MINUTES

**FREEZER-
FRIENDLY**

Set aside a little time on the weekend and whip up a batch of these breakfast sandwiches to enjoy on busy mornings. They're so easy to unwrap, pop in the microwave, and reheat.

Nonstick cooking spray

6 large eggs

⅓ cup milk

Salt

Ground black pepper

6 English muffins

6 precooked sausage patties or cooked bacon, Canadian bacon, or ham slices

6 American cheese slices

1. Preheat the oven to 375°F. Spray a 9-by-13-inch glass baking dish with nonstick cooking spray.

2. In a medium mixing bowl, whisk together the eggs and milk. Season with salt and pepper and whisk again, combining thoroughly. Pour into the prepared baking dish.

3. Bake for 15 to 20 minutes, until cooked through. Remove from the oven. Cut the eggs into six squares.

4. Open the English muffins and place on a baking sheet. Bake for 8 to 10 minutes to toast.

5. On half of each English muffin, place one piece of breakfast meat, one egg square, a piece of cheese, and the top of the English muffin. Wrap each sandwich individually in aluminum foil. Place them all in a zip-top freezer bag, add a note about what's in the bag, and freeze for up to a month.

6. To reheat, unwrap a sandwich and place it on a paper towel–lined microwave-safe plate. Microwave on high for 1½ to 2 minutes, until heated through. Discard the paper towel and enjoy.

~~~~~~

VARIATION: You can use biscuits instead of English muffins. (Try the Easy Homemade Biscuits on page 145.)

PER SERVING CALORIES: 328; TOTAL FAT: 15G; SATURATED FAT: 5G; CHOLESTEROL: 241MG; SODIUM: 731MG; CARBOHYDRATES: 30G; FIBER: 2G; PROTEIN: 19G

Mini Sausage, Egg, and Cheese Frittatas

SERVES 6

PREP TIME:
10 MINUTES

COOK TIME:
20 MINUTES,
PLUS 5 MINUTES
TO COOL

FREEZER-FRIENDLY

GF
GLUTEN-FREE

ONE

These have everything you need for a satisfying breakfast in a compact package. Make them ahead and refrigerate for easy morning meals—just pop one or two in the microwave for 30 seconds to reheat. If gluten is an issue for you, read the label carefully on the precooked sausages. Gluten can lurk in unexpected places.

Nonstick cooking spray

1 (8-ounce) package precooked
    chicken breakfast sausage

6 large eggs

⅓ cup milk

Salt

Ground black pepper

¾ cup sharp Cheddar cheese

1. Preheat the oven to 350°F. Spray the cups of a 12-muffin pan with nonstick cooking spray.

2. Halve the sausages lengthwise, then cut into ½-inch pieces. Divide evenly among the muffin cups.

3. In a medium mixing bowl, whisk together the eggs, milk, salt, and pepper until light and frothy. Ladle into the muffin cups, dividing equally. Sprinkle with Cheddar cheese. Bake for 15 to 18 minutes, until set.

4. Let cool for about 5 minutes before loosening with a knife and removing the mini frittatas. Enjoy immediately.

5. To freeze, wrap individually in aluminum foil, store in a zip-top freezer bag, and freeze for up to a month.

6. To reheat, unwrap a frittata, place on a microwave-safe plate, and microwave on high for 1 to 1½ minutes. Enjoy.

~~~~~~

VARIATION: Try adding a little broccoli or some thinly sliced scallions to the eggs before baking for a little added flavor and nutrition.

PER SERVING CALORIES: 223; TOTAL FAT: 17G; SATURATED FAT: 6G; CHOLESTEROL: 287MG; SODIUM: 382MG; CARBOHYDRATES: 2G; FIBER: 0G; PROTEIN: 16G

TOMATO-GARLIC ROASTED ASPARAGUS, PAGE 44

3

EASY APPETIZERS AND SIDES

Crostini

SERVES 4 TO 6

PREP TIME:
5 MINUTES

COOK TIME:
5 MINUTES

30-MINUTE

ONE

VEGAN

Crostini means "little toasts" in Italian; they're small, thin slices of toasted bread often brushed with a little olive oil or topped with something savory. These crisp little toasts are perfect for the starters that follow in this chapter, and for any other topping that appeals to you. Day-old bread is an absolute must for this recipe; fresh bread will take much longer to cook and may not dry out and crisp up properly in the oven.

1 day-old baguette, cut into ¼-inch-thick slices

Nonstick cooking spray

1. Preheat the oven to 375°F.

2. Spread the baguette slices in a single layer on a baking sheet. Spray with nonstick cooking spray.

3. Bake for 3 to 5 minutes, until crisp but not browned, and enjoy.

VARIATION: You can substitute ciabatta bread for the baguette, but a loaf that's smaller in diameter is best.

PER SERVING CALORIES: 139; TOTAL FAT: 1G; SATURATED FAT: 0G; CHOLESTEROL: 0MG; SODIUM: 312MG; CARBOHYDRATES: 27G; FIBER: 1G; PROTEIN: 6G

Easy Egg Salad

This easy egg salad with a pleasant, smoky flavor is delicious served on crisp Crostini (page 30). For a gluten-free alternative, try serving this on gluten-free crackers or in halved mini sweet peppers (seeds removed, of course).

SERVES 4

PREP TIME:
10 MINUTES

30-MINUTE

GF
GLUTEN-FREE

NO-COOK

ONE

VEGETARIAN

4 large hard-boiled eggs

2 tablespoons mayonnaise

½ teaspoon dry ground mustard

¼ teaspoon garlic powder

¼ teaspoon smoked paprika

Salt

Ground black pepper

Crostini (page 30), gluten-free crackers, or halved and seeded sweet peppers, for serving

1. In a medium mixing bowl, mash the hard-boiled eggs with a potato masher or a large fork.

2. Stir in the mayonnaise, dry mustard, garlic powder, and paprika. Taste, and season with salt and pepper.

3. Spread on crostini, gluten-free crackers, or sweet peppers and serve.

MAKE IT EASIER: You can buy hard-boiled eggs in the refrigerated section of your supermarket. They are sometimes called "hard-cooked," which better describes how they are made.

PER SERVING CALORIES: 101; TOTAL FAT: 7G; SATURATED FAT: 2G; CHOLESTEROL: 213MG; SODIUM: 122MG; CARBOHYDRATES: 2G; FIBER: 0G; PROTEIN: 6G

Tomato and Feta Crostini

SERVES 4 TO 6

PREP TIME:
5 MINUTES

30-MINUTE

NO-COOK

ONE

VEGETARIAN

For this fresh and bright dish, the cheese and tomato mixture is best served in a bowl beside the crostini so the juices don't soak in and make the toasts soggy. Spoon some onto each slice as you go.

Zest of 1 lemon

¼ cup crumbled feta cheese

2 plum tomatoes, finely diced

¼ teaspoon dried oregano

Salt

Ground black pepper

Crostini (page 30), for serving

1. In a medium mixing bowl, stir together the lemon zest, feta, tomatoes, and oregano, and season with salt and pepper.

2. Serve with crostini on the side.

VARIATION: You can substitute 1 teaspoon of finely chopped fresh oregano for the dried oregano.

PER SERVING CALORIES: 169; TOTAL FAT: 3G; SATURATED FAT: 2G; CHOLESTEROL: 8MG; SODIUM: 418MG; CARBOHYDRATES: 29G; FIBER: 2G; PROTEIN: 7G

Brie, Apple, and Prosciutto Crostini

SERVES 6

PREP TIME:
15 MINUTES

Sweet apple, creamy Brie, and salty prosciutto contrast beautifully on a toasty, crispy crostini. If you're going gluten-free, you can just eat these on their own as delicious bites—no crostini needed.

30-MINUTE

NO-COOK

ONE

1 golden delicious apple

1 Brie wedge

3 ounces thinly sliced prosciutto

Crostini (page 30)

1. Core the apple and cut into ¼-inch-thick slices.

2. Cut the Brie into ¼-inch-thick slices. Cut each slice into pieces about 1 inch wide.

3. Cut the prosciutto into 1- to 1½-inch-wide strips, each about 4 inches long.

4. Place one piece of Brie on one apple slice, and wrap with a piece of prosciutto. Repeat with the remaining apple slices and pieces of Brie and prosciutto.

5. Enjoy with crostini.

PER SERVING CALORIES: 176; TOTAL FAT: 6G; SATURATED FAT: 5G; CHOLESTEROL: 5MG; SODIUM: 242MG; CARBOHYDRATES: 22G; FIBER: 1G; PROTEIN: 5G

Herb-Baked Ricotta Dip

SERVES 6

PREP TIME:
5 MINUTES

COOK TIME:
5 MINUTES

Dried herbs and piquant Parmesan cheese flavor this creamy ricotta dip (or spread if you prefer). It's perfect to serve with crostini. Ricotta can be a challenge to stir, so take it slow and push the spoon through the mixture to combine everything.

30-MINUTE

ONE

VEGETARIAN

1 (15-ounce) container
   ricotta cheese

½ teaspoon dried basil

½ teaspoon dried oregano

½ teaspoon dried rosemary

½ cup plus 1 tablespoon grated
   Parmesan cheese, divided

½ teaspoon salt

Crostini (page 30) or chips,
   for dipping

1. In a small, broiler-safe baking dish, combine the ricotta, basil, oregano, rosemary, ½ cup of Parmesan cheese, and salt. Stir well to combine. Spread in an even layer in the baking dish. Sprinkle with the remaining 1 tablespoon of Parmesan cheese.

2. Preheat the broiler on high for 1 minute. Put the dish under the broiler and broil for 4 to 5 minutes, until the ricotta mixture is golden and bubbly at the edges.

3. Serve with crostini or chips for dipping.

VARIATION: For a gluten-free version of this dish, try making crostini with gluten-free bread. This can also be served with sliced fresh vegetables, such as radishes, carrots, cucumbers, and bell peppers.

PER SERVING CALORIES: 247; TOTAL FAT: 12G; SATURATED FAT: 7G; CHOLESTEROL: 42MG; SODIUM: 575MG; CARBOHYDRATES: 21G; FIBER: 1G; PROTEIN: 15G

Greek Salad

I adore the flavors in this salad—cool cucumbers, sweet red bell peppers, salty kalamata olives, and feta cheese, plus tart lemon juice. It's something I could eat daily and never tire of. This easy salad is great on its own as a starter, or as a side salad with grilled or baked chicken.

SERVES 4

PREP TIME:
10 MINUTES, PLUS
10 MINUTES TO
REST

1 cucumber, peeled and diced

1 red bell pepper, seeded and diced

½ cup kalamata olives, chopped

½ cup crumbled feta cheese

1 tablespoon freshly squeezed lemon juice

Salt

Ground black pepper

1. In a large mixing bowl, stir together the cucumber, bell pepper, olives, feta, and lemon juice, and season with salt and pepper.

2. Let sit for 10 minutes before serving, so the flavors can blend.

30-MINUTE

GF
GLUTEN-FREE

NO-COOK

ONE

VEGETARIAN

VARIATION: Add a diced tomato for even more great flavor.

PER SERVING CALORIES: 87; TOTAL FAT: 6G; SATURATED FAT: 3G; CHOLESTEROL: 17MG; SODIUM: 397MG; CARBOHYDRATES: 7G; FIBER: 2G; PROTEIN: 4G

Spinach Salad with Roasted Grapes

SERVES 4

PREP TIME:
10 MINUTES

COOK TIME:
30 MINUTES

GF
GLUTEN-FREE

ONE

V
VEGAN

If you haven't tried roasted grapes, you're missing something wonderful. They are delightful balls of sweetness in this lovely salad. You'll find some homemade vinaigrette options in chapter 9, or use a store-bought bottle.

2 cups seedless grapes

1 tablespoon extra-virgin olive oil

½ teaspoon dried rosemary

Salt

Ground black pepper

4 cups baby spinach

2 tablespoons pepitas (roasted pumpkin seeds)

Vinaigrette of your choice

1. Preheat the oven to 425°F.

2. Spread the grapes on a baking sheet. Drizzle with the olive oil and season with the rosemary, salt, and pepper. Slide into the oven and roast for 25 to 30 minutes, until blistered. Remove and cool slightly.

3. Divide the spinach evenly among four plates. Top with the grapes and pepitas. Drizzle with vinaigrette and serve immediately.

PER SERVING CALORIES: 161; TOTAL FAT: 10G; SATURATED FAT: 1G; CHOLESTEROL: 0MG; SODIUM: 92MG; CARBOHYDRATES: 17G; FIBER: 2G; PROTEIN: 4G

Crispy Panko-Crusted Broccoli

Earthy broccoli gets a nutty flavor when roasted. And it's delightful with this tangy, crispy mixture of lemon and breadcrumbs.

SERVES 4

PREP TIME:
5 MINUTES

COOK TIME:
20 MINUTES

30-MINUTE

ONE

V

VEGAN

2 broccoli heads (about 6 cups), broken into florets

2 tablespoons extra-virgin olive oil

1 tablespoon freshly squeezed lemon juice

Salt

Ground black pepper

¼ cup panko breadcrumbs

1. Preheat the oven to 375°F.

2. In a large mixing bowl, toss together the broccoli, olive oil, and lemon juice, and season with salt and pepper. Arrange in a single layer on a large nonstick baking sheet. Sprinkle with the panko.

3. Bake for 15 to 20 minutes, until browned, and serve.

VARIATION: To make this dish gluten-free, use gluten-free panko breadcrumbs.

PER SERVING CALORIES: 134; TOTAL FAT: 8G; SATURATED FAT: 1G; CHOLESTEROL: 0MG; SODIUM: 119MG; CARBOHYDRATES: 14G; FIBER: 4G; PROTEIN: 5G

Roasted Parmesan Green Beans

SERVES 4 TO 6

PREP TIME:
5 MINUTES

COOK TIME:
30 MINUTES

Tender and ever-so-slightly sweet, roasted green beans are delightful with a crispy Parmesan topping. These are best made with fresh green beans. Frozen ones tend to be too moist for this recipe.

GF
GLUTEN-FREE

ONE

VEGETARIAN

1 pound fresh green beans

Nonstick cooking spray

Salt

Ground black pepper

½ cup freshly grated
   Parmesan cheese

1. Preheat the oven to 400°F.

2. Spread the green beans on a baking sheet. Spray with nonstick cooking spray, and season with salt and pepper.

3. Bake for 20 minutes. Stir.

4. Sprinkle with the Parmesan cheese. Roast for an additional 5 to 10 minutes, until golden, and serve.

MAKE IT EASIER: Short on time? Pick up freshly grated Parmesan from your grocery's cheese section instead of grating your own.

PER SERVING CALORIES: 89; TOTAL FAT: 4G; SATURATED FAT: 2G; CHOLESTEROL: 11MG; SODIUM: 222MG; CARBOHYDRATES: 9G; FIBER: 4G; PROTEIN: 7G

Garlic-Ginger Carrots

Rich with the flavors of garlic and ginger, these carrots disappear fast when I serve them. They are a great accompaniment to many family dinners. If gluten is a concern, look for gluten-free soy sauce or tamari.

SERVES 4

PREP TIME:
10 MINUTES

COOK TIME:
25 MINUTES

GF
GLUTEN-FREE

ONE

VEGAN

3 cups chopped carrots (cut into ¾-inch to 1-inch pieces)

1 tablespoon extra-virgin olive oil

1 teaspoon freshly grated ginger

2 garlic cloves, minced

½ teaspoon salt

1 tablespoon soy sauce

1. Preheat the oven to 400°F.

2. In a large mixing bowl, stir together the carrots, olive oil, ginger, garlic, and salt. Spread it out on a nonstick baking sheet.

3. Bake for 15 to 20 minutes, stirring once or twice. Drizzle with the soy sauce, and toss to coat. Return to the oven, bake for an additional 5 minutes, and serve.

MAKE IT EASIER: Puréed ginger is available both frozen and in the refrigerated section of the supermarket and is an easy alternative to grating your own.

PER SERVING CALORIES: 75; TOTAL FAT: 4G; SATURATED FAT: 1G; CHOLESTEROL: 0MG; SODIUM: 609MG; CARBOHYDRATES: 10G; FIBER: 3G; PROTEIN: 1G

Gingery Glazed Roasted Brussels Sprouts with Red Onion

SERVES 4

PREP TIME:
10 MINUTES

COOK TIME:
30 MINUTES

GLUTEN-FREE

ONE

VEGAN

Roasting Brussels sprouts gives them a pleasant tenderness and hint of sweetness that is divine combined with the soy sauce and ginger glaze. I dare you to resist eating them all from the pan as soon as they come out of the oven!

4 cups Brussels sprouts, quartered

1 small red onion

1 tablespoon extra-virgin olive oil

Salt

Ground black pepper

1 tablespoon soy sauce or tamari (gluten-free if needed)

1 tablespoon seasoned rice vinegar

1 teaspoon freshly grated ginger

1. Preheat the oven to 400°F.

2. Spread the Brussels sprouts on a nonstick baking sheet. Quarter the red onion, then halve each quarter. Spread the onion pieces on the baking sheet with the Brussels sprouts. Drizzle with the olive oil, and season liberally with salt and pepper. Toss together.

3. Roast for 15 minutes. Stir, and roast for an additional 5 minutes.

4. In a small mixing bowl, whisk together the soy sauce, rice vinegar, and ginger. Drizzle over the Brussels sprouts, and toss to coat.

5. Roast for 5 to 10 minutes, until well-glazed, and serve.

VARIATION: You can substitute two shallots for the red onion. Peel and quarter the shallots and toss with the Brussels sprouts before roasting.

PER SERVING CALORIES: 79; TOTAL FAT: 4G; SATURATED FAT: 1G; CHOLESTEROL: 0MG; SODIUM: 287MG; CARBOHYDRATES: 10G; FIBER: 4G; PROTEIN: 4G

Rosemary Potato Wedges

Crispy on the outside, soft on the inside—these wedges are a wonderful side dish alongside burgers, sandwiches, chicken, and just about anything.

SERVES 4

PREP TIME:
10 MINUTES

COOK TIME:
30 MINUTES

GF
GLUTEN-FREE

ONE

(V)
VEGAN

1 pound (about 2) russet potatoes

2 tablespoons extra-virgin olive oil

1 teaspoon dried rosemary

1 teaspoon salt

1 teaspoon cornstarch

Ground black pepper

1. Preheat the oven to 425°F. Place a nonstick baking sheet in the oven while it preheats.

2. Cut the potatoes into thin (about ½-inch-wide) wedges. Add to a large mixing bowl.

3. In a small mixing bowl, stir together the olive oil, rosemary, salt, and cornstarch. Drizzle over the potatoes, and toss well to combine.

4. Arrange the potatoes on the hot baking sheet in a single layer. Roast for 15 minutes. Flip and roast for an additional 10 to 15 minutes, until golden.

5. Season with pepper and serve.

PER SERVING CALORIES: 152; TOTAL FAT: 7G; SATURATED FAT: 1G; CHOLESTEROL: 0MG; SODIUM: 578MG; CARBOHYDRATES: 21G; FIBER: 1G; PROTEIN: 2G

Garlic-Parsley Sweet Potato Fries

SERVES 4

PREP TIME:
15 MINUTES

COOK TIME:
40 MINUTES

GF
GLUTEN-FREE

VEGAN

Roasted sweet potatoes are delicious, but even more so when mixed with the sharp flavor of garlic and herbaceous parsley. What I love best about this recipe is that even proclaimed sweet potato haters can be swayed by the flavors and fry shapes.

1 pound sweet potatoes, cut into ½-inch-thick fry shapes

3 tablespoons extra-virgin olive oil, divided

1 teaspoon salt, plus more for seasoning

½ teaspoon ground black pepper, plus more for seasoning

1 garlic clove, minced

1 tablespoon finely chopped fresh parsley

1. Preheat the oven to 425°F. Place a nonstick baking sheet in the oven while it's preheating.

2. In a large mixing bowl, combine the sweet potatoes, 2 tablespoons of olive oil, and the salt and pepper. Stir vigorously to combine. Arrange the fries on the hot nonstick baking sheet, taking care to arrange them in a single layer.

3. Return the pan to the oven and roast for 35 to 40 minutes, flipping the fries once or twice during that time. They are done when the sweet potatoes are fork-tender and browned.

4. In a small skillet over medium heat, heat the remaining 1 tablespoon of olive oil. Add the garlic and cook, stirring, for 1 minute, until fragrant. Pour over the fries.

5. Sprinkle with the parsley, and toss well. Taste, season with more salt and pepper as desired, and serve.

MAKE IT EASIER: Preheating the pan in the oven results in a crisper outside for the sweet potatoes, since they start cooking on contact. You can skip this step, if you prefer, and instead line the baking sheet with nonstick aluminum foil.

PER SERVING CALORIES: 188; TOTAL FAT: 10G; SATURATED FAT: 1G; CHOLESTEROL: 0MG; SODIUM: 645MG; CARBOHYDRATES: 23G; FIBER: 3G; PROTEIN: 2G

Tomato-Garlic Roasted Asparagus

SERVES 4

PREP TIME:
5 MINUTES

COOK TIME:
15 MINUTES

Crisp-tender roasted asparagus is topped with bright tomatoes and garlic in this quick and easy side dish. Although I love the whisper-thin spears of the first asparagus in the spring, this dish is best made with thicker, slightly more mature asparagus spears.

30-MINUTE

GF
GLUTEN-FREE

ONE

V
VEGAN

1 asparagus bunch, ends trimmed

1 cup halved grape tomatoes

2 garlic cloves, minced

1 tablespoon extra-virgin olive oil

Salt

Ground black pepper

1. Preheat the oven to 400°F.

2. Cut the asparagus into 3-inch pieces. Arrange on a nonstick baking sheet. Top with the grape tomatoes and garlic. Drizzle with the olive oil, and sprinkle with salt and pepper. Toss to combine.

3. Roast for 10 to 15 minutes, until crisp-tender, and serve.

VARIATION: You can substitute a minced shallot for the garlic, for a bit of a different flavor.

PER SERVING CALORIES: 52; TOTAL FAT: 4G; SATURATED FAT: 1G; CHOLESTEROL: 0MG; SODIUM: 16MG; CARBOHYDRATES: 5G; FIBER: 2G; PROTEIN: 2G

Mini Crab Cake Bites

Packed with crab and laced with garlic flavor, these mini crab cake bites are tender on the inside and crisp on the outside—a perfect appetizer to share. Go easy on the salt here; you shouldn't need more than a pinch or so.

SERVES 4

PREP TIME:
5 MINUTES

COOK TIME:
15 MINUTES

30-MINUTE

ONE

1 (6-ounce) can crabmeat, drained and picked over

1 shallot, finely chopped

⅓ cup breadcrumbs

½ teaspoon garlic powder

Salt

Ground black pepper

2 tablespoons mayonnaise

2 tablespoons extra-virgin olive oil

1. Preheat the oven to 375°F.

2. In a large mixing bowl, stir together the crabmeat, shallot, breadcrumbs, and garlic powder. Season lightly with salt and pepper. Stir in the mayonnaise. Using your hands, form 10 (1-inch) balls.

3. In a large, oven-safe skillet over medium heat, heat the olive oil. Add the crab cake balls to the pan and brown on all sides, 3 to 4 minutes total.

4. Slide the pan into the oven and bake for 10 minutes.

5. Let cool for a few minutes before transferring to a serving dish.

VARIATION: You can substitute fresh crabmeat for canned. Either way, you'll have to pick through the crab to remove any bits of shells.

PER SERVING CALORIES: 172; TOTAL FAT: 10G; SATURATED FAT: 1G; CHOLESTEROL: 34MG; SODIUM: 276MG; CARBOHYDRATES: 9G; FIBER: 0G; PROTEIN: 11G

CILANTRO-LIME QUINOA SALAD WITH SWEET POTATOES, PAGE 54

VEGAN AND VEGETARIAN MAINS

Easy Tomato and Black Bean Soup

SERVES 4

PREP TIME:
10 MINUTES

COOK TIME:
15 MINUTES

30-MINUTE

**FREEZER-
FRIENDLY**

GF
GLUTEN-FREE

ONE

VEGAN

Cumin gives this satisfying soup an earthy, nutty, warm flavor with a hint of spice. The tomatoes and black beans give it a good bulk, too. For a heartier meal, serve this soup with a side salad or warm, buttery cheese quesadilla.

1 (14.5-ounce) can petite-diced tomatoes (not drained)

1 (15.5-ounce) can black beans, drained and rinsed

2 cups water

½ cup finely diced red bell peppers

1 teaspoon ground cumin

Salt

Ground black pepper

1 tablespoon finely chopped fresh cilantro

1. In a medium saucepan over medium heat, stir together the tomatoes and their juices, the black beans, water, bell peppers, cumin, and a sprinkling of salt and pepper. Cover the pot, and cook for 15 minutes. Stir.

2. Add the cilantro and stir well. Taste, adjust the seasonings, and serve.

3. This soup freezes well. Simply store in freezer-safe containers. Defrost in the refridgerator overnight, and reheat on the stove in a saucepan over medium heat.

VARIATION: Not a fan of black beans? White cannellini beans are great, too.

PER SERVING CALORIES: 136; TOTAL FAT: 1G; SATURATED FAT: 0G; CHOLESTEROL: 0MG; SODIUM: 7MG; CARBOHYDRATES: 25G; FIBER: 9G; PROTEIN: 9G

Quick Thai Red Curry with Vegetables

Creamy and warming, this is delicious served over a bed of rice or quinoa. This curry has a bite. Use full-fat coconut milk for best results, and be sure to season with additional salt, pepper, and cilantro as needed.

SERVES 4

PREP TIME:
5 MINUTES

COOK TIME:
25 MINUTES

30-MINUTE

GLUTEN-FREE

ONE

(V)
VEGAN

1 (13.5-ounce) can coconut milk
2 tablespoons Thai red curry paste
1 tablespoon light brown sugar
Salt

Ground black pepper
2 (16-ounce) bags frozen stir-fry vegetables
1 tablespoon finely chopped fresh cilantro

1. In a large sauté pan over medium heat, combine the coconut milk, curry paste, and brown sugar. Heat, stirring until combined. Taste, and season with salt and pepper. Bring to a boil, then reduce the heat to medium-low. Simmer for 5 minutes.

2. Stir in the frozen stir-fry vegetables. Cover, increase the heat to medium, and cook for 10 to 15 minutes, until the vegetables are defrosted.

3. Stir in the cilantro, taste, adjust the seasonings, and serve.

VARIATION: You can substitute 4 cups of fresh vegetables for frozen ones. Some vegetables may need additional cooking time and/or may need to be precooked before adding.

PER SERVING CALORIES: 314; TOTAL FAT: 25G; SATURATED FAT: 22G; CHOLESTEROL: 0MG; SODIUM: 67MG; CARBOHYDRATES: 23G; FIBER: 5G; PROTEIN: 6G

Vegetable Fried Rice

SERVES 4

PREP TIME:
15 MINUTES

COOK TIME:
15 MINUTES

Filled with veggies and good flavor, this dish is quick to make and so satisfying. It's an egg-free fried rice, but I love to serve it with a poached or fried egg.

30-MINUTE

GF
GLUTEN-FREE

ONE

VEGAN

2 tablespoons extra-virgin olive oil

1 yellow onion, diced

1 cup grated carrot

1 cup finely shredded green cabbage

Salt

Ground black pepper

1 tablespoon sesame oil (optional)

2 cups cooked rice

2 tablespoons soy sauce or tamari (gluten-free if needed)

1. In a large skillet over medium heat, heat the olive oil.

2. Add the onion, carrot, and cabbage to the skillet. Season with salt and pepper. Cook, stirring occasionally, until softened and lightly browned, 10 to 15 minutes.

3. Push the veggies to the side of the skillet. Add the sesame oil (if using), then add the rice and stir into the sesame oil for 1 minute. Combine with the veggies. Mix thoroughly.

4. Remove from the heat, and drizzle with the soy sauce. Stir well. Season again with salt and pepper and serve.

MAKE IT EASIER: When you're making rice this week, cook some extra so you'll have it all ready to use in this recipe.

PER SERVING CALORIES: 185; TOTAL FAT: 7G; SATURATED FAT: 1G; CHOLESTEROL: 0MG; SODIUM: 527MG; CARBOHYDRATES: 29G; FIBER: 2G; PROTEIN: 4G

Angel Hair Pasta with Garlic Spinach

Fans of aglio olio, the comforting Italian dish of garlic pasta, will love this take on it. A hearty pop of baby spinach gives it a bright dimension. Angel hair pasta generally cooks in 3 to 5 minutes, but it can vary, so it's a really good idea to check the package and time your pasta accordingly.

SERVES 6

PREP TIME:
5 MINUTES

COOK TIME:
10 MINUTES

30-MINUTE

V
VEGAN

1 pound angel hair pasta

⅓ cup extra-virgin olive oil

4 to 5 garlic cloves, minced

2 cups baby spinach, chopped

Salt

Ground black pepper

1. Cook the angel hair pasta according to package directions. Drain well. Transfer back to the pot.

2. In a small skillet over medium heat, heat the olive oil. Add the garlic and cook, stirring once or twice, until fragrant but not browned, about 1 to 2 minutes.

3. Pour the olive oil and garlic over the pasta in the pot. Toss well. Add the spinach and toss again.

4. Season with salt and pepper and serve.

VARIATION: For a cheesy version of this pasta, add ¼ cup freshly grated Romano cheese at the same time as the spinach.

PER SERVING CALORIES: 390; TOTAL FAT: 13G; SATURATED FAT: 2G; CHOLESTEROL: 0MG; SODIUM: 13MG; CARBOHYDRATES: 57G; FIBER: 3G; PROTEIN: 10G

Twice-Baked Sweet Potatoes with Onion, Garlic, and Spinach

SERVES 4

PREP TIME:
10 MINUTES

COOK TIME:
1 HOUR,
15 MINUTES

GF
GLUTEN-FREE

VEGAN

The natural sweetness of sweet potatoes is a lovely contrast to the savory stuffing ingredients. While this dish takes a long time to cook, the quick and easy prep means very little hands-on time.

4 large sweet potatoes

1 tablespoon extra-virgin olive oil

1 medium yellow onion, diced

Salt

Ground black pepper

2 cups baby spinach, chopped

4 garlic cloves, minced

1. Preheat the oven to 400°F.

2. Prick the sweet potatoes along the tops 3 to 4 times with a fork. Place them in the oven on the top rack with a baking sheet on a rack below them. Bake 40 to 50 minutes, or until fork-tender. Set aside to cool.

3. When you're ready to stuff and bake the potatoes, preheat the oven to 400°F again.

4. Halve the sweet potatoes lengthwise. Scoop the insides into a medium mixing bowl and mash thoroughly. Set aside the scooped-out skins.

5. In a large skillet over medium heat, heat the olive oil. Add the onion, and season with salt and pepper. Cook, stirring occasionally, until they are beginning to brown, about 8 minutes. Add to the mashed sweet potatoes in the bowl, along with the spinach and garlic. Stir well to combine. Season with salt and pepper.

6. Scoop the sweet potato mixture back into the skins. Place on a baking sheet and bake for 10 to 15 minutes, until hot, and serve.

MAKE IT EASIER: You can bake the sweet potatoes the first time and store them in the refrigerator uncut up to 2 days in advance.

PER SERVING CALORIES: 161; TOTAL FAT: 4G; SATURATED FAT: 1G; CHOLESTEROL: 0MG; SODIUM: 85MG; CARBOHYDRATES: 30G; FIBER: 5G; PROTEIN: 3G

Cilantro-Lime Quinoa Salad with Sweet Potatoes

SERVES 4

PREP TIME:
10 MINUTES

COOK TIME:
35 MINUTES,
PLUS 5 MINUTES
TO REST

GF
GLUTEN-FREE

VEGAN

It's the contrasts in this salad that make it delightful: the sugary sweetness of the sweet potatoes, the tang of the lime juice, the earthy flavor of the cilantro. Though it can be enjoyed hot or cold, we like it best hot.

1 sweet potato (about ¾ pound),
   cut into ½-inch chunks

1 shallot, quartered and
   roughly chopped

1 tablespoon extra-virgin olive oil

Salt

Ground black pepper

1 cup quinoa, thoroughly rinsed

2 cups water

Zest and juice of 1 lime

2 tablespoons finely chopped
   fresh cilantro

1. Preheat the oven to 400°F.

2. Spread the diced sweet potatoes and shallot in an 8-by-8-inch square glass baking dish. Drizzle with the olive oil, and season with salt and pepper. Bake for 20 minutes. Stir well. Return to the oven and bake for an additional 10 to 15 minutes, until the sweet potatoes are fork-tender.

3. Meanwhile, in a medium saucepan over high heat, stir together the quinoa and water. Bring to a boil, reduce the heat to low, cover, and cook for 15 minutes, or until the water is absorbed. Turn off the heat and let sit for 5 minutes.

4. In a large serving bowl, stir together the quinoa, sweet potatoes, and shallots. Add the lime juice, lime zest, and cilantro. Stir well.

5. Taste, season as needed with additional salt and pepper, and serve.

MAKE IT EASIER: You can find fresh chopped cilantro in the produce section and frozen in little cubes in the freezer section. Both make quick work of adding herbs to dishes like this.

PER SERVING CALORIES: 216; TOTAL FAT: 6G; SATURATED FAT: 1G; CHOLESTEROL: 0MG; SODIUM: 21MG; CARBOHYDRATES: 34G; FIBER: 4G; PROTEIN: 7G

Spaghetti Squash Pomodoro

SERVES 4

PREP TIME:
10 MINUTES

COOK TIME:
30 MINUTES

GF
GLUTEN-FREE

ONE

VEGAN

This is one of my very favorite vegan dinners. Roasted spaghetti squash shreds into spaghetti-like tendrils and is then topped with a fresh, bright tomato sauce.

1 spaghetti squash

Nonstick cooking spray

2 cups (about 2 medium) diced fresh tomatoes

1 garlic clove, minced

1 tablespoon finely chopped fresh basil

Salt

Ground black pepper

1. Preheat the oven to 375°F.

2. Halve the spaghetti squash lengthwise. Scoop out and discard the seeds and stringy insides. Spray with nonstick cooking spray. Place each half cut-side down on a baking sheet. Bake for 30 minutes, or until the squash can easily be pricked with a fork.

3. Meanwhile, in a medium mixing bowl, stir together the tomatoes, garlic, and basil. Season with salt and pepper, and set aside.

4. Once the spaghetti squash is cooked, scrape a fork across the inside cavity to shred the squash into spaghetti-like threads. Continue until you reach the shell.

5. To serve, divide the spaghetti squash evenly among four plates. Top each one with a quarter of the tomato mixture.

~~~~~~

VARIATION: After shredding the spaghetti squash, put it back inside the shell and top each half with half of the tomato mixture. Serve in the shell on serving dishes. Also, you can substitute canned diced tomatoes for the fresh tomatoes. Drain before adding them in step 3.

PER SERVING CALORIES: 64; TOTAL FAT: 1G; SATURATED FAT: 0G; CHOLESTEROL: 0MG; SODIUM: 30MG; CARBOHYDRATES: 14G; FIBER: 1G; PROTEIN: 2G

French Bread Pizza

SERVES 4

PREP TIME:
10 MINUTES

COOK TIME:
15 MINUTES

30-MINUTE

ONE

VEGETARIAN

After a long, tiring day, this is one of those recipes that can make quick work of dinner. Drop by the grocery store for ingredients, and whip it up in less than 30 minutes. Change up the toppings to fit your taste. Red or green bell pepper slices, olives, pineapple, and artichoke hearts all make great toppings, and if you're not vegetarian, sausage, pepperoni, sliced meatballs, and ham chunks work, too. Better yet, have everyone make their own and then just bake!

1 baguette

1 cup Easy Tomato Marinara (page 143) or any marinara sauce

1 cup shredded mozzarella cheese

¼ cup thinly sliced red onions

¼ cup diced tomatoes

1. Preheat the oven to 375°F.

2. Cut the baguette into four pieces, then slice each one open, separating the top and bottom halves.

3. Arrange on a baking sheet. Top with the marinara sauce, mozzarella cheese, onions, and tomatoes.

4. Bake for 10 to 15 minutes, until the cheese is melted and the bread is heated throughout, and serve.

MAKE IT EASIER: Head to the salad bar at your local grocery and choose whatever toppings you want. They're already chopped and cut, so you can just make the pizzas and bake.

PER SERVING CALORIES: 297; TOTAL FAT: 8G; SATURATED FAT: 4G; CHOLESTEROL: 22MG; SODIUM: 590MG; CARBOHYDRATES: 43G; FIBER: 3G; PROTEIN: 15G

Tomato and Roasted Red Pepper Soup

Rich and slightly sweet, this soup is perfect for chilly days. Want to make it even better and more filling? Serve it with grilled cheese sandwiches for dipping.

SERVES 4 TO 6

PREP TIME:
10 MINUTES

COOK TIME:
25 MINUTES

GF
GLUTEN-FREE

ONE

VEGETARIAN

1 tablespoon extra-virgin olive oil

2 garlic cloves, minced

1 (14.5-ounce) can diced tomatoes (not drained)

1 (12-ounce) jar roasted red peppers, drained and roughly chopped

1 teaspoon dried thyme

2 cups water

½ cup heavy (whipping) cream

Salt

Ground black pepper

1. In a medium saucepan, heat the olive oil. Add the garlic. Cook and stir for 1 minute, or until fragrant.

2. Add the tomatoes and their juices and the roasted red peppers, thyme, and water. Stir well. Bring to a boil.

3. Reduce the heat to medium-low, cover, and simmer for 15 minutes. Remove from the heat.

4. Using an immersion blender or a blender (be sure to vent it), purée completely. Stir in the heavy cream.

5. Taste, season with salt and pepper, and serve.

VARIATION: Try serving this soup with chopped microgreens and a sprinkling of Parmesan cheese for a pretty (and tasty) presentation.

PER SERVING CALORIES: 174; TOTAL FAT: 15G; SATURATED FAT: 7G; CHOLESTEROL: 41MG; SODIUM: 18MG; CARBOHYDRATES: 10G; FIBER: 2G; PROTEIN: 2G

Stuffed Tomatoes

SERVES 4

PREP TIME:
10 MINUTES

COOK TIME:
40 MINUTES

ONE

VEGETARIAN

Bread lovers will appreciate these tomatoes, stuffed with bread-crumbs, diced tomato, garlic, and cheese. The butter mixed in gives it all a lovely richness.

4 medium tomatoes

⅔ cup seasoned breadcrumbs

2 garlic cloves, minced

½ cup grated Parmesan cheese

¼ cup unsalted butter, melted

Salt

Ground black pepper

1. Preheat the oven to 375°F.

2. Slice the tops off the tomatoes. Scoop out the insides. You want to get all the watery bits, the seeds, and much of the flesh in the center, leaving a solid ¼-inch or more shell of the tomato. Discard the seeds and watery bits. Turn the tomatoes upside down on a paper towel to drain.

3. Meanwhile, dice the tops and any other solid bits to make 1 cup diced tomatoes.

4. In a medium mixing bowl, mix together the diced tomato bits, breadcrumbs, garlic, cheese, and melted butter. Season lightly with salt and pepper.

5. Stuff the breadcrumb mixture into the tomatoes.

6. Place the tomatoes in an 8-by-8-inch glass baking dish. Bake for 35 to 40 minutes, until the stuffing is golden brown, and serve.

PER SERVING CALORIES: 250; TOTAL FAT: 16G; SATURATED FAT: 10G; CHOLESTEROL: 42MG; SODIUM: 410MG; CARBOHYDRATES: 19G; FIBER: 2G; PROTEIN: 8G

Tortellini Caprese

Fresh tomatoes, creamy mozzarella, and bright basil combine with satisfying tortellini in this easy pasta dish that can be served warm or chilled. Start with either fresh or frozen tortellini.

SERVES 4

PREP TIME:
10 MINUTES

COOK TIME:
15 MINUTES

30-MINUTE

ONE

VEGETARIAN

1 (10-ounce) package cheese tortellini

1½ cups grape tomatoes, halved

¾ cup fresh mozzarella pearls or fresh mozzarella, cut into ½-inch chunks

½ cup thinly sliced fresh basil

1 tablespoon extra-virgin olive oil

Salt

Ground black pepper

1. Heat a medium saucepan of water to boiling over high heat. Cook the tortellini according to the package directions.

2. Meanwhile, in a large mixing bowl, stir together the grape tomatoes, mozzarella, and basil.

3. When the tortellini is done, drain and rinse with cool water. Drain thoroughly. Add to the tomato mixture and mix well.

4. Drizzle with the olive oil, and season with salt and pepper. Stir again and serve.

VARIATION: Change up the flavor in this dish by choosing different varieties of tortellini or tortelloni (bigger tortellini).

PER SERVING CALORIES: 319; TOTAL FAT: 13G; SATURATED FAT: 6G; CHOLESTEROL: 46MG; SODIUM: 376MG; CARBOHYDRATES: 36G; FIBER: 2G; PROTEIN: 15G

Spinach-Artichoke Baked Ravioli

SERVES 4 TO 6

PREP TIME:
5 MINUTES

COOK TIME:
35 MINUTES

Creamy cheese ravioli are baked with fresh spinach, meaty artichoke hearts, and bright tomatoes and topped with mozzarella cheese in this easy dinner casserole. The ravioli cook up perfectly right from frozen in the oven.

ONE

VEGETARIAN

1 (24-ounce) bag frozen cheese ravioli

1 cup baby spinach, chopped

1 (14-ounce) can quartered artichoke hearts, drained and chopped

1 (14.5-ounce) can diced tomatoes (not drained)

1 tablespoon extra-virgin olive oil

Salt

Ground black pepper

1 cup shredded mozzarella cheese

1. Preheat the oven to 375°F.

2. Place the ravioli in an 8-by-8-inch baking dish.

3. Add the baby spinach and artichoke hearts to the baking dish along with the tomatoes and their juices, olive oil, salt, and pepper. Stir well to combine. Sprinkle with the mozzarella cheese.

4. Tent a piece of aluminum foil over the baking dish, securing the edges. Bake for 25 minutes. Remove the foil and cook for an additional 10 minutes, or until bubbly around the edges, and serve.

VARIATION: For more spinach flavor, use spinach and cheese ravioli.

PER SERVING CALORIES: 495; TOTAL FAT: 19G; SATURATED FAT: 7G; CHOLESTEROL: 62MG; SODIUM: 754MG; CARBOHYDRATES: 63G; FIBER: 5G; PROTEIN: 22G

Cheesy Eggplant-Tomato Casserole

I love this method of cooking eggplant: The eggplant is cooked alone first and then used in a flavorful, layered dish with cheese and tomatoes.

SERVES 4

PREP TIME:
5 MINUTES

COOK TIME:
1 HOUR,
15 MINUTES

VEGETARIAN

1 eggplant (about 1 pound), peeled and cut into ¼-inch-thick slices

½ teaspoon salt

Ground black pepper

4 teaspoons seasoned breadcrumbs, divided

1 (14.5-ounce) can diced tomatoes (not drained), divided

1 cup shredded mozzarella cheese, divided

1 tablespoon grated Parmesan cheese

1. Preheat the oven to 375°F.

2. Arrange the eggplant slices on a baking sheet, and sprinkle with the salt and a dash of pepper. Bake for 15 to 20 minutes, until tender.

3. Arrange the baked eggplant slices in a single layer in the bottom of an 8-by-8-inch baking dish. Sprinkle with 1 teaspoon of breadcrumbs, one-third of the tomatoes with their juices, and one-third of the mozzarella cheese. Repeat to create three layers. Top with the Parmesan cheese and the remaining 1 teaspoon of breadcrumbs.

4. Cover with aluminum foil and bake for 40 minutes. Remove the foil and bake for an additional 10 to 15 minutes, until the top is bubbly and the cheese is melted, and serve.

VARIATION: You can substitute diced fresh tomatoes for the canned tomatoes.

PER SERVING CALORIES: 142; TOTAL FAT: 7G; SATURATED FAT: 4G; CHOLESTEROL: 23MG; SODIUM: 217MG; CARBOHYDRATES: 12G; FIBER: 5G; PROTEIN: 9G

Roasted Broccoli and Carrot Quinoa with Browned Butter

SERVES 4

PREP TIME:
10 MINUTES

COOK TIME:
30 MINUTES,
PLUS 5 MINUTES
TO REST

GF
GLUTEN-FREE

VEGETARIAN

The nuttiness of the roasted broccoli and browned butter is lovely with the sweet roasted carrots and bright basil. The quinoa, which is a veritable blank canvas for dishes like this, makes the dish as filling as it is satisfying.

1 cup quinoa, thoroughly rinsed

2 cups water

4 cups fresh broccoli florets

1 cup finely diced carrot

1 tablespoon extra-virgin olive oil

Salt

Ground black pepper

3 tablespoons unsalted butter

2 tablespoons fresh basil, thinly sliced

1. Preheat the oven to 400°F.

2. In a medium saucepan over high heat, combine the quinoa and water and bring to a boil. Reduce the heat to low, cover, and simmer for 15 minutes.

3. Meanwhile, as the quinoa simmers, arrange the broccoli florets and carrots on a large baking sheet. Drizzle with the olive oil, and season with salt and pepper. Roast for 15 to 20 minutes, stirring once or twice, until the broccoli is browned in spots.

4. When the quinoa is finished simmering, remove from the heat and let it sit, covered, for 5 minutes.

5. In a large mixing bowl, combine the cooked quinoa and the broccoli mixture. Stir well.

6. In a small skillet over medium heat, melt the butter. Continue cooking, stirring often, until it begins to brown, 2 to 3 minutes. You want the rich, golden-brown color to spread through the butter. Then immediately remove it from the heat and pour over the quinoa mixture.

7. Add the basil and stir well. Taste, season with additional salt and pepper, and serve.

VARIATION: You can substitute couscous, prepared according to the package directions, for the quinoa. (The dish will not be gluten-free.)

PER SERVING CALORIES: 306; TOTAL FAT: 15G; SATURATED FAT: 6G; CHOLESTEROL: 23MG; SODIUM: 115MG; CARBOHYDRATES: 36G; FIBER: 6G; PROTEIN: 9G

Parmesan-Leek Quiche

SERVES 6

PREP TIME:
10 MINUTES, PLUS
10 MINUTES TO
SOAK

COOK TIME:
55 MINUTES

**FREEZER-
FRIENDLY**

VEGETARIAN

If my daughter had her way, there would be a quiche for her to dig into every day in our house. This one, with slightly sweet leeks and nutty Parmesan cheese, is one she absolutely adores. It's airy, fragrant, and perfect for brunch, lunch, or even dinner. Serve it with a green salad. Also, it reheats well. Just place a slice on a microwave-safe plate and microwave for 1 to 2 minutes.

1 leek, halved lengthwise and
    thinly sliced

1 tablespoon extra-virgin olive oil

1 frozen deep-dish piecrust

1 cup freshly grated Parmesan cheese

5 large eggs

1 cup milk

½ teaspoon salt

1. Preheat the oven to 375°F.

2. Put the leeks in a medium mixing bowl and fill with water. Swish around. Soak for 10 minutes to remove dirt. Drain well.

3. In a large skillet over medium heat, heat the olive oil. Add the leeks and cook, stirring, until softened, 10 to 12 minutes.

4. Pour the leeks into the piecrust, evenly distributing them. Spread the Parmesan over them.

5. In a large mixing bowl, whisk together the eggs, milk, and salt until well combined. Pour into the piecrust. Bake for 35 to 45 minutes, until set, slice, and serve.

6. To freeze the leftovers, cut into slices and set them out on a wax paper–lined baking sheet that you place in the freezer. When they're frozen, wrap each individually, place in a freezer-friendly container, and freeze for up to 4 months. To reheat, defrost in the refrigerator overnight. Microwave on high for 1 to 2 minutes, until hot.

VARIATION: You can substitute a homemade piecrust for the frozen one. Just be sure to use a deep-dish pie plate.

PER SERVING CALORIES: 317; TOTAL FAT: 20G; SATURATED FAT: 8G; CHOLESTEROL: 185MG; SODIUM: 450MG; CARBOHYDRATES: 19G; FIBER: 1G; PROTEIN: 15G

TERIYAKI SALMON AND AVOCADO BOWL WITH PICKLED RADISHES, PAGE 72

5

FISH AND SEAFOOD MAINS

Smoked Salmon and Avocado Wrap

SERVES 1

PREP TIME:
10 MINUTES

30-MINUTE

NO-COOK

ONE

A good wrap can be so satisfying. This one—filled with smoked salmon, creamy avocado, and crunchy vegetables—is quick, easy, and perfect for lunch or dinner. And of course, you can easily multiply the ingredient quantities by the number of wraps you'd like to make to serve up as many as you'd like.

1 tortilla

3 ounces sliced smoked salmon

½ avocado, sliced

4 or 5 thin cucumber slices

1 or 2 thin red onion slices

1. Lay out the tortilla on a cutting board. Lay the smoked salmon along the center, followed by the avocado, cucumber, and red onion slices.

2. Fold the ends of the wrap in, then roll up to close. Cut in half and enjoy.

VARIATION: You can use warm cooked salmon instead of smoked salmon. Just flake the salmon with a fork before adding it to the wrap.

PER SERVING CALORIES: 374; TOTAL FAT: 18G; SATURATED FAT: 3G; CHOLESTEROL: 19MG; SODIUM: 959MG; CARBOHYDRATES: 34G; FIBER: 7G; PROTEIN: 21G

Honey-Lime-Ginger Salmon

When we have little time for dinner, salmon is such an easy and convenient option to get on the table. It cooks so quickly, and my kids and I adore it. Sweet, tart, and gingery, this salmon is lovely served with rice and a salad.

SERVES 4

PREP TIME:
5 MINUTES

COOK TIME:
20 MINUTES

1 (1-pound) salmon fillet

1 tablespoon honey

1 tablespoon freshly squeezed
   lime juice

1 teaspoon freshly grated ginger

Salt

Ground black pepper

30-MINUTE

GF
GLUTEN-FREE

ONE

1. Preheat the oven to 400°F. Line a baking sheet with aluminum foil.

2. Place the salmon on the baking sheet. In a small mixing bowl, whisk together the honey, lime juice, and ginger. Brush half of the mixture onto the salmon. Season with salt and pepper.

3. Bake the salmon for 12 to 15 minutes, until just opaque. Remove from the oven and brush with the remaining honey-lime-ginger mixture. Return to the oven and cook for an additional 4 to 5 minutes, until fork-tender.

4. Cut into four pieces and serve.

MAKE IT EASIER: You can use 4 (4-ounce) salmon fillets or a 1-pound piece of salmon without changing anything in the recipe.

PER SERVING CALORIES: 179; TOTAL FAT: 7G; SATURATED FAT: 1G; CHOLESTEROL: 62MG; SODIUM: 50MG; CARBOHYDRATES: 5G; FIBER: 0G; PROTEIN: 23G

Teriyaki Salmon and Avocado Bowl with Pickled Radishes

SERVES 4

PREP TIME:
10 MINUTES

COOK TIME:
20 MINUTES

30-MINUTE

GLUTEN-FREE

On a trip to Boston over the winter, my kids and I picked up sushi bowls at Boston Public Market to enjoy while we waited for the bus home to leave. They were an absolute delight with a variety of flavors and textures. And that's what inspired this dish. Creamy avocado, tangy pickled radishes, and a sweet teriyaki salmon glaze come together in this rice bowl for a satisfying and delicious dinner.

½ cup (about 4 to 5) thinly sliced radishes

6 teaspoons seasoned rice vinegar, divided

Salt

1 pound salmon, cut into 4 (4-ounce) fillets

Ground black pepper

¼ cup teriyaki sauce

4 cups cooked rice

2 avocados, peeled, pitted, and thinly sliced

1. Preheat the oven to 400°F.

2. In a small mixing bowl, stir together the radishes and 2 teaspoons of rice vinegar. Season lightly with salt. Let sit, stirring a few times, for at least 20 minutes.

3. Meanwhile, arrange the salmon fillets on a baking sheet. Season liberally with salt and pepper. Bake for 10 to 12 minutes, until opaque. Remove from the oven and brush thoroughly with the teriyaki sauce. Return to the oven and cook for an additional 5 to 6 minutes, until cooked through.

4. Divide the rice evenly among four bowls. Drizzle each with 1 teaspoon of the remaining rice vinegar, and season with salt. Top with one-quarter of the avocado and one-quarter of the pickled radishes.

5. Using a fork, flake the salmon fillets one at a time, transferring the salmon from each fillet to one of the prepared rice bowls, and serve.

MAKE IT EASIER: Want perfect, thin radish slices? It's easy if you have the right tools. A mandoline is a cutting tool that makes quick work of slicing the radishes extra thin.

PER SERVING CALORIES: 489; TOTAL FAT: 18G; SATURATED FAT: 3G; CHOLESTEROL: 62MG; SODIUM: 754MG; CARBOHYDRATES: 50G; FIBER: 6G; PROTEIN: 30G

Easy Fish Tacos

SERVES 4

PREP TIME:
5 MINUTES

COOK TIME:
20 MINUTES

30-MINUTE

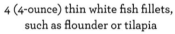

GF
GLUTEN-FREE

ONE

Tacos are a dinner my kids and I can always agree on. The fresh flavors in these warm tacos are also perfect for pairing with Easy Pickled Carrots (page 141) or Spicy Pineapple Salsa (page 139).

4 (4-ounce) thin white fish fillets, such as flounder or tilapia

Salt

Ground black pepper

1 to 2 tablespoons extra-virgin olive oil

1 (12-count) package small white corn tortillas

1 avocado, pitted, peeled, and sliced

¼ red onion, thinly sliced

1 lime, cut into wedges, for serving

1. Season the fish fillets with salt and pepper.

2. In a large nonstick skillet over medium heat, heat the olive oil. Add the fish fillets, taking care not to overcrowd the skillet. Cook, flipping once, until the fish is opaque and lightly browned in spots, 5 to 7 minutes total. Transfer to a plate. Repeat, as needed, until all the fish has been cooked.

3. Warm the tortillas according to the package directions.

4. To assemble, divide the fish evenly among the tortillas. Top each with avocado and red onion and serve with a lime wedge.

VARIATION: You can use flour tortillas instead of corn tortillas if you like them better and don't need the tacos to be gluten-free.

PER SERVING CALORIES: 250; TOTAL FAT: 11G; SATURATED FAT: 2G; CHOLESTEROL: 57MG; SODIUM: 73MG; CARBOHYDRATES: 14G; FIBER: 4G; PROTEIN: 25G

Asiago Panko-Crusted Tuna

The first time I made this dish, my daughter and I practically licked our plates. With a cheesy, crunchy topping, this seared tuna is delightful on its own, but it's even better served with a green salad.

SERVES 4

PREP TIME:
5 MINUTES

COOK TIME:
5 MINUTES

30-MINUTE

ONE

1 tablespoon unsalted butter, melted

¼ cup panko breadcrumbs

¼ cup grated Asiago cheese

¼ teaspoon smoked paprika

Salt

Ground black pepper

4 (4-ounce) tuna fillets

1. Put the oven rack at the top of the oven, and preheat the broiler.

2. In a small mixing bowl, stir together the melted butter, panko, Asiago, and paprika. Season with salt and pepper, and set aside.

3. Season the tuna fillets liberally all over with salt and pepper.

4. Heat a large oven-safe nonstick skillet over high heat until hot. Sear the tuna for 1½ minutes per side, flipping once. Top the tuna with the panko mixture, pressing it onto the fillets. Broil for 2 to 3 minutes, until the topping browns.

5. Remove from the oven, immediately transfer the tuna fillets to plates (otherwise they will keep cooking), and serve.

VARIATION: You can substitute Romano cheese for the Asiago.

PER SERVING CALORIES: 200; TOTAL FAT: 6G; SATURATED FAT: 3G; CHOLESTEROL: 63MG; SODIUM: 207MG; CARBOHYDRATES: 5G; FIBER: 0G; PROTEIN: 30G

Crab-Stuffed Portobello Mushrooms

SERVES 4

PREP TIME:
15 MINUTES

COOK TIME:
30 MINUTES

GF
GLUTEN-FREE

ONE

Fresh crabmeat really makes this dish special. Look for lump crabmeat at the seafood counter. And whatever you do, don't substitute imitation crabmeat. It is not the same.

4 large portobello mushrooms (each about 4 inches in diameter), stemmed and finely chopped

8 ounces lump crabmeat, picked over

1 shallot, finely chopped

1 large egg

½ cup freshly grated Romano cheese

Salt

Ground black pepper

Lemon wedges, for serving (optional)

1. Preheat the oven to 375°F. Line a baking sheet with aluminum foil.

2. In a medium mixing bowl, use a metal spoon to scrape out the gills from the mushrooms and discard. Place the mushroom caps open-side up on the baking sheet.

3. In the mixing bowl, stir well to thoroughly combine the crabmeat, shallot, and egg. Stir in the Romano cheese, and season with salt and pepper.

4. Divide the crab mixture evenly among the portobello mushroom caps, pressing it down as you spoon it in.

5. Bake for 25 to 30 minutes, until the filling begins to brown on top. Serve hot with lemon wedges (if using).

~~~~~~

VARIATION: Can't find large portobello mushroom caps? Use 6 medium ones (about 3 inches in diameter) instead.

PER SERVING CALORIES: 150; TOTAL FAT: 6G; SATURATED FAT: 3G; CHOLESTEROL: 94MG; SODIUM: 814MG; CARBOHYDRATES: 5G; FIBER: 1G; PROTEIN: 19G

Easy White Clam Pita Pizzas

SERVES 4

PREP TIME:
10 MINUTES

COOK TIME:
10 MINUTES

30-MINUTE

ONE

These pizzas bring together tastes of the sea (clams) and the land (garlic and cheese), and the flavors blend really well. Building this pizza on pita breads makes quick work of it.

4 pita breads

1 tablespoon extra-virgin olive oil

1 garlic clove, minced

½ cup (or more) shredded mozzarella

1 (6.5-ounce) can minced clams, drained

Salt

1 tablespoon finely chopped fresh parsley

1. Preheat the oven to 375°F. Arrange the pita breads on a baking sheet.

2. In a small mixing bowl, stir together the olive oil and garlic. Brush liberally on the pita breads, taking care to get garlic on all of them.

3. Top each of the pita breads with one-quarter of the mozzarella and one-quarter of the clams. Season with salt.

4. Bake for 5 to 7 minutes, until the cheese is melted. Sprinkle with parsley and serve.

VARIATION: Freshly grated Parmesan or Romano cheese can add an extra dimension to this pizza's flavor. Try some instead of, or in addition to, the mozzarella.

PER SERVING CALORIES: 211; TOTAL FAT: 8G; SATURATED FAT: 3G; CHOLESTEROL: 40MG; SODIUM: 285MG; CARBOHYDRATES: 18G; FIBER: 2G; PROTEIN: 17G

Garlic-Parsley Shrimp

Garlicky and tender, these shrimp are excellent served on salad, over rice, or with pasta. The parsley adds a pleasant, fresh, peppery flavor to this dish.

SERVES 4

PREP TIME:
10 MINUTES

COOK TIME:
10 MINUTES

30-MINUTE

GLUTEN-FREE

ONE

2 tablespoons extra-virgin olive oil

1 pound raw large or extra-large shrimp, peeled and deveined

3 garlic cloves, minced

Salt

Ground black pepper

2 tablespoons finely chopped fresh parsley

1. Heat a large skillet over medium heat.

2. Swirl the olive oil around the pan. Add the shrimp and garlic, and season with salt and pepper. Cook, flipping once, until the shrimp are opaque, about 2 to 3 minutes per side.

3. Remove from the stove and transfer the shrimp to a serving dish. Sprinkle with the parsley and serve.

VARIATION: For a little extra oomph, add a pinch or two of crushed red pepper to the pan while the shrimp is cooking. The shrimp will be a little spicy—but pleasantly so.

MAKE IT EASIER: Look for frozen peeled and deveined shrimp with tails removed in the freezer case. Defrost them by putting the shrimp in a colander under cold running water, shaking the colander a few times during thawing. The shrimp will defrost in about 10 minutes.

PER SERVING CALORIES: 184; TOTAL FAT: 9G; SATURATED FAT: 1G; CHOLESTEROL: 172MG; SODIUM: 169MG; CARBOHYDRATES: 2G; FIBER: 0G; PROTEIN: 23G

Linguine with Lemon-Garlic Clam Sauce

SERVES 6

PREP TIME:
5 MINUTES

COOK TIME:
15 MINUTES

30-MINUTE

FREEZER-FRIENDLY

Tangy, briny, and garlicky—this satisfying pasta is simple to make but impressive to eat. It reheats well, too. My kids love taking these leftovers for lunch.

1 pound linguine

¼ cup extra-virgin olive oil

4 garlic cloves, minced

1 (6.5-ounce) can minced clams in clam juice

¼ cup freshly squeezed lemon juice

⅓ cup chopped fresh parsley

Salt

Ground black pepper

1. Bring a large pot of water to a boil. Cook the linguine according to the package directions.

2. Meanwhile, in a large skillet over medium heat, heat the olive oil. Add the garlic and cook, stirring, until fragrant, 1 to 2 minutes. Pour in the clams and their juices, and continue to stir. Cook for 3 minutes. Remove from the heat.

3. Put the drained pasta back in the pasta pot, and pour the clam mixture over it. Toss well. Drizzle with lemon juice, and toss again. Stir in the parsley. Taste, season with salt and pepper, and serve.

4. Store leftovers in an airtight container in the refrigerator for up to 4 days. Reheat in a microwave-safe bowl for 1 to 2 minutes on high. To freeze, store individual portions in freezer-friendly containers in the freezer for up to 4 months. Defrost in the refrigerator overnight. To reheat, place in a microwave-safe bowl and microwave on high for 2 to 3 minutes, until heated through.

PER SERVING CALORIES: 408; TOTAL FAT: 11G; SATURATED FAT: 2G; CHOLESTEROL: 19MG; SODIUM: 39MG; CARBOHYDRATES: 60G; FIBER: 3G; PROTEIN: 17G

Parmesan Shrimp and Broccoli Pasta

SERVES 6

PREP TIME:
10 MINUTES

COOK TIME:
20 MINUTES

Shrimp lovers will love this simple, elegant pasta. An abundance of broccoli makes it a balanced meal, and a hearty sprinkle of Parmesan makes it extra flavorful. You can substitute steamed fresh broccoli for the frozen broccoli.

30-MINUTE

1 (12-ounce) package frozen broccoli florets

1 pound penne pasta

2 tablespoons extra-virgin olive oil

3 garlic cloves, minced

1 pound large shrimp, peeled and deveined

Salt

Ground black pepper

¾ cup freshly grated Parmesan cheese

1. Heat a large pot of water to boiling and cook the broccoli according to the package directions. Set aside.

2. Cook the penne in the same pot (see the Make It Easier tip), according to the package directions.

3. Meanwhile, in a large skillet over medium heat, heat the olive oil. Add the garlic and cook until fragrant, about 1 minute. Add the shrimp and season with salt and pepper. Cook until opaque, 4 to 5 minutes.

4. Drain the cooked pasta thoroughly and return to the pot. Add the shrimp and garlic, the cooked broccoli, and the Parmesan cheese. Mix thoroughly and serve.

~~~~~~

MAKE IT EASIER: Submerge the broccoli in the boiling water using a metal strainer basket. Lift it out when it's cooked, and boil the pasta in the same water.

PER SERVING CALORIES: 471; TOTAL FAT: 11G; SATURATED FAT: 3G; CHOLESTEROL: 126MG; SODIUM: 321MG; CARBOHYDRATES: 61G; FIBER: 4G; PROTEIN: 32G

CHICKEN SNOW PEA SKILLET, PAGE 89

CHICKEN AND TURKEY MAINS

Easy Panko-Crusted Chicken Fingers

SERVES 4

PREP TIME:
5 MINUTES

COOK TIME:
20 MINUTES

30-MINUTE

ONE

Everyone needs a good, basic recipe for chicken. This is it. These crispy chicken fingers are perfect for dipping in your favorite sauce or salsa.

1 pound raw chicken tenders

Salt

Ground black pepper

½ cup panko breadcrumbs

1. Preheat the oven to 425°F.

2. Season the chicken on both sides with salt and pepper. Then place it in a zip-top bag with the panko. Shake well to coat.

3. Arrange in a single layer on a nonstick baking sheet. Bake for 15 to 20 minutes, or until the chicken is cooked through, and serve.

VARIATION: For a spicy take on this recipe, sprinkle the chicken with a little cayenne pepper powder before tossing it in the panko.

PER SERVING CALORIES: 178; TOTAL FAT: 2G; SATURATED FAT: 1G; CHOLESTEROL: 66MG; SODIUM: 197MG; CARBOHYDRATES: 10G; FIBER: 1G; PROTEIN: 28G

Crispy Chicken Drumsticks

These are my kids' very favorite. They bake up crispy on the outside, juicy on the inside. When they are done cooking, you can also toss them with a favorite sauce before digging in. I particularly like a mix of teriyaki and barbecue sauce.

SERVES 4

PREP TIME:
15 MINUTES

COOK TIME:
50 MINUTES

ONE

Nonstick cooking spray

⅓ cup all-purpose flour

1 teaspoon salt

½ teaspoon ground black pepper

½ teaspoon smoked paprika

1½ pounds (about 6) chicken drumsticks

1. Preheat the oven to 475°F. Spray a 9-by-13-inch glass baking dish with nonstick cooking spray.

2. In a small, flat-bottom bowl, stir together the flour, salt, pepper, and paprika. Dredge the chicken drumsticks in the flour mixture, and place them in the prepared baking dish.

3. Bake for 40 to 50 minutes, until the chicken is golden and cooked through, and serve.

PER SERVING CALORIES: 264; TOTAL FAT: 12G; SATURATED FAT: 0G; CHOLESTEROL: 112MG; SODIUM: 952MG; CARBOHYDRATES: 8G; FIBER: 1G; PROTEIN: 28G

Chicken Cordon Bleu Sandwiches

SERVES 4

PREP TIME:
10 MINUTES

COOK TIME:
25 MINUTES

The first time I had chicken cordon bleu—breaded chicken stuffed with ham and creamy cheese—it seemed so fancy. It came from a meat market and was unlike anything I'd ever had before. This sandwich is like a classic chicken cordon bleu turned inside out. It's so satisfying and easy.

ONE

Nonstick cooking spray

1 pound thin-cut chicken breasts

Salt

¼ cup seasoned breadcrumbs

4 deli ham slices

4 deli provolone cheese slices

4 rolls, sliced open

1. Preheat the oven to 425°F. Spray a nonstick baking sheet with nonstick cooking spray.

2. Put the breadcrumbs in a small, flat-bottom bowl. If the chicken breasts are large, cut them in half. You should have 4 breast pieces. Season on both sides with salt, then dredge in the seasoned breadcrumbs. Place on the baking sheet, and spray with additional nonstick cooking spray.

3. Bake for 20 minutes. Top each chicken piece with a slice of ham and then a slice of provolone cheese. Bake for an additional 3 to 4 minutes, until the cheese is melted.

4. Place a chicken breast in each roll, and serve.

VARIATION: You can use Swiss cheese in place of provolone.

PER SERVING CALORIES: 373; TOTAL FAT: 13G; SATURATED FAT: 4G; CHOLESTEROL: 103MG; SODIUM: 953MG; CARBOHYDRATES: 25G; FIBER: 2G; PROTEIN: 38G

Chicken Snow Pea Skillet

Serve this easy, garlicky stir-fry with rice or mashed potatoes. Other vegetables, such as shallots and asparagus, will be delicious in this recipe as well.

SERVES 4

PREP TIME:
10 MINUTES

COOK TIME:
15 MINUTES

30-MINUTE

ONE

1 pound boneless chicken breast or tenderloins, cut into 1-inch pieces

1 tablespoon all-purpose flour

Salt

Ground black pepper

2 tablespoons extra-virgin olive oil

2 garlic cloves, minced

1½ cups snow peas, cut into 1-inch pieces

½ cup finely diced carrot

1. In a medium mixing bowl, toss together the chicken, flour, and a sprinkle of salt and pepper until the chicken is thoroughly coated.

2. In a large skillet over medium heat, heat the olive oil. Add the chicken and cook until it is opaque on all sides, 3 to 4 minutes total.

3. Add the garlic to the skillet, and stir to combine. Cook for 1 minute, or until fragrant. Add the snow peas and carrots. Stir well. Cover and cook for 10 minutes more, stirring once.

4. Uncover and stir. Taste, season with salt and pepper, and serve.

MAKE IT EASIER: Check for prechopped fresh veggies in the produce department, or mine the salad bar for options.

PER SERVING CALORIES: 247; TOTAL FAT: 10G; SATURATED FAT: 1G; CHOLESTEROL: 72MG; SODIUM: 108MG; CARBOHYDRATES: 11G; FIBER: 3G; PROTEIN: 27G

Mediterranean Chicken Skillet

SERVES 4

PREP TIME:
10 MINUTES

COOK TIME:
20 MINUTES

In Maine, tomatoes start appearing in farmers' markets toward the end of August or in early September. That's when they are at their peak flavor—and take a fresh and tangy dish like this from really good to absolutely great.

30-MINUTE

GF

GLUTEN-FREE

ONE

2 tablespoons extra-virgin olive oil

1 pound boneless chicken breast, cubed

Salt

Ground black pepper

1 cup diced fresh tomatoes

2 garlic cloves, minced

1 shallot, finely minced

¼ cup finely chopped fresh basil

1 tablespoon balsamic vinegar

1. In a large nonstick skillet over medium heat, heat the olive oil. Add the chicken breast, and season with salt and pepper. Stir well, cooking until browned on all sides, 15 to 20 minutes.

2. Meanwhile, in a medium mixing bowl, stir together the tomatoes, garlic, shallot, basil, and vinegar. Season with salt and pepper.

3. When the chicken is cooked through, add the tomato mixture and toss well. Remove from the heat and enjoy immediately.

VARIATION: This skillet is easily transformed into a pasta dish. Just toss with 1 pound of cooked pasta (gluten-free pasta, if you prefer) dressed with a little olive oil.

PER SERVING CALORIES: 278; TOTAL FAT: 15G; SATURATED FAT: 1G; CHOLESTEROL: 0MG; SODIUM: 41MG; CARBOHYDRATES: 7G; FIBER: 1G; PROTEIN: 28G

Sheet Pan Hawaiian Chicken

Sheet pan dinners are wonderful because everything cooks together at the same time. Sweet and savory, this dish is perfect served over rice.

SERVES 4

PREP TIME:
10 MINUTES

COOK TIME:
25 MINUTES

GF
GLUTEN-FREE

ONE

1 pound thin-cut chicken breasts

1 (20-ounce) can pineapple chunks in juice

1 red bell pepper, seeded and cut into strips

1 tablespoon extra-virgin olive oil

Salt

Ground black pepper

¼ cup soy sauce or tamari (gluten-free, if needed)

1 tablespoon freshly grated ginger

1. Preheat the oven to 400°F.

2. Arrange the chicken on a nonstick baking sheet. Drain the pineapple, reserving the juice. Place the pineapple chunks and red pepper strips on and around the chicken. Drizzle with olive oil, and season with salt and pepper. Bake for 20 minutes.

3. Meanwhile, in a small mixing bowl, whisk together the soy sauce, 2 to 3 tablespoons of reserved pineapple juice, and the ginger.

4. Brush the mixture all over the chicken, pineapple, and peppers, bake for an additional 5 to 7 minutes, and serve.

VARIATION: You can use any color of bell pepper in this recipe. Sliced red onions will also taste great.

PER SERVING CALORIES: 233; TOTAL FAT: 5G; SATURATED FAT: 1G; CHOLESTEROL: 65MG; SODIUM: 1,015MG; CARBOHYDRATES: 23G; FIBER: 3G; PROTEIN: 28G

Sticky Raspberry-Lime Chicken Drumsticks

SERVES 4

PREP TIME:
10 MINUTES

COOK TIME:
25 MINUTES, PLUS
10 MINUTES TO
COOL

GF
GLUTEN-FREE

ONE

The first time I made these, my kids demolished them. The sticky glaze makes them a sweet-tangy delight.

2 pounds (about 5 or 6) chicken drumsticks

Salt

Ground black pepper

⅓ cup seedless raspberry jam or preserves

2 tablespoons freshly squeezed lime juice

3 to 6 drops hot sauce, plus more if desired

1. Preheat the oven to 475°F.

2. Pat the chicken with a paper towel to ensure it's as dry as possible all over. Season generously on all sides with salt and pepper. Arrange on a nonstick baking sheet, and bake for 10 minutes.

3. While the chicken is baking, in a small mixing bowl, whisk together the raspberry jam and lime juice. Add 3 to 6 drops of hot sauce, and season with salt. Taste and adjust the seasoning.

4. Remove the chicken from the oven, flip the pieces, then baste liberally with the raspberry-lime mixture. Bake for another 10 minutes.

5. Take the chicken out again, flip, and baste again with the remaining glaze mixture. Bake for 5 minutes more.

6. Let cool for 10 minutes before enjoying.

VARIATION: You can substitute apricot jam for the raspberry.

PER SERVING CALORIES: 377; TOTAL FAT: 18G; SATURATED FAT: 5G; CHOLESTEROL: 190MG; SODIUM: 408MG; CARBOHYDRATES: 19G; FIBER: 0G; PROTEIN: 36G

Honey-Sesame Chicken Thighs

SERVES 4

PREP TIME:
10 MINUTES

COOK TIME:
25 MINUTES

GF
GLUTEN-FREE

ONE

Chicken thighs are a more flavorful cut of chicken than the breasts. But that comes at a cost—you do need to spend some time trimming them of fat, because they often have a lot (yes, even the already trimmed ones). But the payoff is a lightly glazed chicken dinner that's lovely served with rice and steamed vegetables.

1 pound boneless chicken thighs, trimmed of fat

1 tablespoon extra-virgin olive oil

Salt

Ground black pepper

1 tablespoon honey

½ teaspoon seasoned rice vinegar

½ teaspoon soy sauce or tamari (gluten-free, if needed)

1 teaspoon sesame seeds

1. Preheat the oven to 425°F.

2. Arrange the chicken thighs in an 8-by-8-inch glass baking dish. Drizzle with the olive oil, and sprinkle with salt and pepper. Bake for 20 minutes.

3. In a small mixing bowl, whisk together the honey, rice vinegar, and soy sauce. Brush all over the chicken. Sprinkle with the sesame seeds, bake for an additional 5 minutes, and serve.

VARIATION: You can use thin-cut chicken breasts in place of chicken thighs. The cooking time will remain the same.

PER SERVING CALORIES: 291; TOTAL FAT: 21G; SATURATED FAT: 6G; CHOLESTEROL: 95MG; SODIUM: 164MG; CARBOHYDRATES: 5G; FIBER: 0G; PROTEIN: 20G

Smothered Chicken Breasts with Caramelized Onions and Provolone

SERVES 4

PREP TIME:
10 MINUTES

COOK TIME:
35 MINUTES,
PLUS 5 MINUTES
TO REST

GF
GLUTEN-FREE

It's the sweet caramelized onions in this dish that transform it from good to magical. This recipe has a few more steps than most in this book, but it's still pretty easy. It's also excellent for serving on special occasions or to guests.

1½ pounds boneless chicken breasts

1 teaspoon dried basil

Salt

Ground black pepper

2 tablespoons extra-virgin olive oil

2 yellow onions, halved and thinly sliced

1 tablespoon balsamic vinegar

¼ pound sliced deli provolone cheese

1. Preheat the oven to 400°F.

2. Place the chicken breasts on a baking sheet, and rub the basil, salt, and pepper all over them. Bake for 20 to 25 minutes, until cooked through.

3. Meanwhile, in a large skillet over medium-low heat, heat the olive oil. Add the onions, and season with salt and pepper. Cook, stirring occasionally, until golden brown, 20 to 25 minutes. Drizzle with balsamic vinegar, and stir well. Cook for an additional 2 to 3 minutes, until the vinegar is absorbed.

4. Remove the chicken from the oven and let sit for 5 minutes. Cut the chicken breasts into ¼-inch slices. Arrange in an oven-safe serving dish (or baking dish). Top with the onions and then the provolone. Bake for 2 to 3 minutes more, until the cheese is melted, and serve.

~~~~~~

VARIATION: Serve the chicken on rolls, with onions and cheese piled on top.

PER SERVING CALORIES: 495; TOTAL FAT: 26G; SATURATED FAT: 6G; CHOLESTEROL: 22MG; SODIUM: 228MG; CARBOHYDRATES: 12G; FIBER: 1G; PROTEIN: 49G

Turkey-Veggie Wraps

SERVES 1

PREP TIME:
10 MINUTES

30-MINUTE

NO-COOK

ONE

This is just a really good turkey wrap. I like to wrap mine in either aluminum foil or plastic wrap before I cut it in half, so it holds its shape and doesn't unroll. (You'll find some homemade vinaigrette options in chapter 9, or use a store-bought bottle.)

1 tortilla wrap

4 ounces boneless turkey breast (leftovers from a turkey or sliced deli meat—both work)

½ cup spring greens mix or lettuce of your choice

¼ cucumber, thinly sliced

2 tablespoons finely diced red bell pepper

1 teaspoon vinaigrette or any dressing you love (optional)

1. Lay out the wrap on a cutting board. In the center, arrange the turkey breast in a line, then the greens, cucumber, and bell pepper. Drizzle with the dressing (if using).

2. Fold the ends in and roll up to close. Cut in half and enjoy.

VARIATION: For more substance and flavor, you can add some sliced avocado to this wrap. You can also use a gluten-free wrap to make it gluten-free.

PER SERVING CALORIES: 238; TOTAL FAT: 5G; SATURATED FAT: 1G; CHOLESTEROL: 50MG; SODIUM: 987MG; CARBOHYDRATES: 20G; FIBER: 3G; PROTEIN: 33G

Turkey Bacon Pita Pockets

This quick and easy dinner is perfect for those busy nights. This is the kind of recipe I turn to when we're all running in different directions and just need to eat something fast.

SERVES 4

PREP TIME:
5 MINUTES

COOK TIME:
10 MINUTES

30-MINUTE

ONE

8 bacon slices

4 pita pockets

8 ounces turkey slices (sliced deli meat or leftover turkey)

1 avocado, pitted, peeled, and sliced

1 cup shredded or torn lettuce

1. In a large skillet over medium heat, cook the bacon on both sides until crisp, about 8 minutes total. Drain on a paper towel–lined plate.

2. Cut open the pita pockets. Divide the turkey evenly among the pockets. Then add the bacon, avocado, and lettuce, and serve.

PER SERVING CALORIES: 520; TOTAL FAT: 26G; SATURATED FAT: 7G; CHOLESTEROL: 85MG; SODIUM: 1,132MG; CARBOHYDRATES: 34G; FIBER: 4G; PROTEIN: 36G

Bacon-Wrapped Turkey-Cheddar Rollups

SERVES 4

PREP TIME:
10 MINUTES

COOK TIME:
30 MINUTES

GF
GLUTEN-FREE

ONE

Forget Thanksgiving; this turkey is bold and brilliant. Sharp Cheddar and salty, crisp bacon conspire to make this an unforgettable and impressive meal. You can substitute any cheese that melts well for the Cheddar.

4 turkey breast cutlets (about 1 pound total)

Salt

Ground black pepper

2 tablespoons shredded Cheddar cheese

4 bacon slices

1. Preheat the oven to 400°F.

2. Season the turkey breast cutlets with salt and pepper on both sides.

3. On the end of each cutlet, sprinkle ¼ of the Cheddar cheese. Roll up the breast lengthwise. Wrap the cutlet with the bacon.

4. In an oven-safe skillet set over medium heat, brown the four rollups on all sides, about 2 minutes per side. Slide the skillet into the oven and bake until cooked through, 15 to 20 minutes, and serve.

MAKE IT EASIER: Having trouble keeping the bacon in place? Use a wooden toothpick or two to secure the rollup. Be sure to remove them before eating.

PER SERVING CALORIES: 248; TOTAL FAT: 11G; SATURATED FAT: 3G; CHOLESTEROL: 25MG; SODIUM: 500MG; CARBOHYDRATES: 0G; FIBER: 0G; PROTEIN: 35G

Seasoned Turkey Cutlets

The secret to these juicy, flavorful turkey cutlets is the mayonnaise that binds the garlic and herbs on top. This dish is easy enough for any night, but also elegant enough that it could make a great alternative to a whole bird on Thanksgiving.

SERVES 4

PREP TIME:
5 MINUTES

COOK TIME:
25 MINUTES

30-MINUTE

GF
GLUTEN-FREE

ONE

2 tablespoons mayonnaise

1 garlic clove, minced

1 teaspoon dried thyme

1 teaspoon dried rosemary

1 teaspoon salt

4 turkey breast cutlets (about
1 pound total)

1. Preheat the oven to 375°F.

2. In a small mixing bowl, stir together the mayonnaise, garlic, thyme, rosemary, and salt. Set aside.

3. Arrange the turkey cutlets on a nonstick baking sheet and spread with the mayonnaise mixture.

4. Bake for 20 to 25 minutes, until cooked through and golden brown, and serve.

VARIATION: Top with a little panko breadcrumbs before baking for a crispy-top version of this dish. Use gluten-free breadcrumbs if needed.

PER SERVING CALORIES: 163; TOTAL FAT: 5G; SATURATED FAT: 0G; CHOLESTEROL: 2MG; SODIUM: 634MG; CARBOHYDRATES: 2G; FIBER: 0G; PROTEIN: 27G

Herb-Garlic Turkey Tenderloin

SERVES 6

PREP TIME:
5 MINUTES

COOK TIME:
40 MINUTES,
PLUS 10 MINUTES
TO REST

Tenderloins are long, often wide pieces of boneless turkey breast meat cut from the center of the two breasts. This turkey tenderloin produces a juicy, tender meat with a robust flavor. Wonderful right from the oven, it is also excellent thinly sliced and added to sandwiches, wraps, and salads.

GF
GLUTEN-FREE

ONE

1 pound turkey tenderloin

1 tablespoon extra-virgin olive oil

2 garlic cloves, minced

½ teaspoon dried oregano

½ teaspoon dried basil

Salt

Ground black pepper

1. Preheat the oven to 400°F.

2. Place the turkey tenderloin in a 9-by-13-inch glass baking dish. Brush all over with the olive oil. Sprinkle with the garlic, oregano, and basil, and season with salt and pepper.

3. Bake for 35 to 40 minutes, or until a meat thermometer inserted into the center of the tenderloin reads 160°F and the meat is pale and mostly white with mostly clear juices.

4. Remove from the oven and let rest for 10 minutes before slicing and serving.

VARIATION: Try serving slices of this turkey on a Caesar salad.

PER SERVING CALORIES: 102; TOTAL FAT: 3G; SATURATED FAT: 0G; CHOLESTEROL: 30 MG; SODIUM: 71MG; CARBOHYDRATES: 0G; FIBER: 0G; PROTEIN: 19G

Slow Cooker Smoked Paprika Turkey Breast

Whole turkeys are labor-intensive to make, but with a slow cooker, the turkey becomes pretty hands-off. This is how I often cook our turkey for Thanksgiving. Don't have a slow cooker? Try the recipe for Herb-Garlic Turkey Tenderloin (page 100), which cooks in the oven.

SERVES 6

PREP TIME:
20 MINUTES

COOK TIME:
7 HOURS, PLUS
15 MINUTES TO
REST

GF
GLUTEN-FREE

ONE

1 bone-in split turkey breast (about 2 to 3 pounds total), skinless

1 tablespoon unsalted butter, melted

½ teaspoon smoked paprika

½ teaspoon dried oregano, basil, or thyme

Salt

Ground black pepper

1. Place the split turkey breast in the bowl of a slow cooker. Brush with the melted butter. Season with the smoked paprika, oregano, salt, and pepper.

2. Cover and cook on low for 5 to 7 hours, until cooked through.

3. Remove from the slow cooker and let sit for 15 minutes before slicing and serving.

MAKE IT EASIER: To remove the skin from the turkey breast, slide your hand under the skin to loosen it. Pull it away, using a small knife to cut places where it's stubbornly attached, until it's fully removed.

PER SERVING CALORIES: 178; TOTAL FAT: 20G; SATURATED FAT: 6G; CHOLESTEROL: 145MG; SODIUM: 161MG; CARBOHYDRATES: 0G; FIBER: 0G; PROTEIN: 48G

EASY STEAK TACOS, PAGE 107

7

BEEF AND PORK MAINS

Barbecue Roasted Beef Wrap

SERVES 2

PREP TIME:
10 MINUTES

30-MINUTE

NO-COOK

ONE

When my son's track team returns from a meet after 8 p.m., this is the dinner I have waiting for him. Roast beef with barbecue sauce is a winning combination. It's easy to toss together and so satisfying.

2 tortilla wraps

¼ pound deli roast beef slices

1 plum tomato, sliced

2 tablespoons shredded Cheddar cheese

2 tablespoons barbecue sauce

1. Lay the wraps on a cutting board. Arrange the roast beef, tomatoes, and Cheddar on top of one wrap. They should be layered beginning at the edge of the wrap and continuing to the center. Leave one side of the wrap untopped. Drizzle the topped side with barbecue sauce.

2. Fold the untopped end of the wrap over the toppings and then roll into a cylinder. Enjoy.

MAKE IT EASIER: I wrap these up in foil or plastic wrap to help them keep their shape while eating. Just roll back the foil or plastic wrap as you go.

VARIATION: Use gluten-free tortilla wraps to make this meal gluten-free.

PER SERVING CALORIES: 320; TOTAL FAT: 12G; SATURATED FAT: 5G; CHOLESTEROL: 55 MG; SODIUM: 495MG; CARBOHYDRATES: 30G; FIBER: 2G; PROTEIN: 21G

Easy Skillet Burgers

Well-seasoned burgers are a cinch to make on the stove. Adjust the cooking time to achieve your desired doneness, cooking longer for well-done burgers. Just leave off the buns if you're going gluten-free, or choose a gluten-free bread.

SERVES 4

PREP TIME:
10 MINUTES

COOK TIME:
20 MINUTES

30-MINUTE

GLUTEN-FREE

ONE

1 pound ground beef

½ teaspoon salt

¼ teaspoon garlic powder

⅛ teaspoon ground black pepper

4 hamburger buns

1. Divide the ground beef into four equal portions. Form into patty shapes about ¼- to ½-inch thick each.

2. In a small mixing bowl, stir together the salt, garlic powder, and pepper. Sprinkle evenly on both sides of all the patties.

3. Heat a large nonstick skillet over medium-high heat. Add the burgers to the skillet and cook for 5 to 8 minutes per side, to desired doneness.

4. Serve on the buns.

VARIATION: Why not cheeseburgers? Top the burgers with a slice of Cheddar, American, or provolone a minute before they come off the stove. The cheese will melt brilliantly.

PER SERVING CALORIES: 298; TOTAL FAT: 15G; SATURATED FAT: 6G; CHOLESTEROL: 71MG; SODIUM: 376 MG; CARBOHYDRATES: 15G; FIBER: 1G; PROTEIN: 24G

Easy Meatballs Marinara

SERVES 4

PREP TIME:
10 MINUTES

COOK TIME:
20 MINUTES

30-MINUTE

**FREEZER-
FRIENDLY**

ONE

These meatballs are simple but comforting. Try making them with your own marinara sauce (my recipe for Easy Tomato Marinara is on page 143) or your favorite store-bought sauce. This meal freezes well either as a whole dish or portioned into individual containers.

1 pound ground beef

¾ cup seasoned breadcrumbs

1 large egg

1 teaspoon garlic powder

1 teaspoon salt

¼ teaspoon ground black pepper

½ tablespoon extra-virgin olive oil

2 cups marinara sauce

1. In a large mixing bowl, stir together the ground beef, breadcrumbs, egg, garlic powder, salt, and pepper. Knead by hand to completely combine the ingredients. Roll into 1-inch balls.

2. In a large skillet over medium heat, heat the olive oil. Add the meatballs and brown on all sides, about 5 minutes total.

3. Pour the marinara sauce over the meatballs. Cover, reduce heat to medium-low, and simmer for 15 minutes. Serve.

4. To freeze, store in plastic containers or zip-top freezer bags for up to 4 months. Defrost overnight in the refrigerator and microwave for 1 to 2 minutes to reheat.

VARIATION: Instead of garlic powder, try adding one minced garlic clove to the meatballs for a zestier flavor. Add to the skillet after the meatballs are browned, and stir for 1 minute. You can also substitute gluten-free breadcrumbs to make this dish gluten-free.

PER SERVING CALORIES: 326; TOTAL FAT: 19G; SATURATED FAT: 7G; CHOLESTEROL: 123 MG; SODIUM: 654MG; CARBOHYDRATES: 14G; FIBER: 0G; PROTEIN: 26G

Easy Steak Tacos

With only 5 minutes of active preparation, this is the perfect dinner for those evenings when you just don't have time to get an elaborate meal on the table. Though these are pretty substantial on their own, a tossed salad is a nice side accompaniment with this recipe.

SERVES 4

PREP TIME:
5 MINUTES

COOK TIME:
25 MINUTES

30-MINUTE

GLUTEN-FREE

ONE

1 red onion, halved and thinly sliced

1 tablespoon extra-virgin olive oil

Salt

Ground black pepper

1 pound sirloin steaks (thin-cut preferred)

1 package small corn tortillas, heated per package directions

1 avocado, peeled, pitted, and cut into chunks

1. Preheat the oven to 400°F.

2. Arrange the onion slices on a nonstick baking sheet, and drizzle with the olive oil. Season with salt and pepper, and roast for 10 minutes.

3. Meanwhile, season the sirloin steaks on both sides with salt and pepper.

4. After 10 minutes, stir the onions, then push them to the ends of the baking sheet. Place the steaks in the center, not touching each other. Roast for 5 minutes. Flip, then roast for an additional 5 to 10 minutes, to desired doneness.

5. Slice the sirloin steak into thin strips. Fill the corn tortillas with the steak, onions, and avocado, and serve.

VARIATION: You can add cheese, such as queso fresco or shredded Cheddar, to the tacos as you're assembling them.

PER SERVING CALORIES: 360; TOTAL FAT: 22G; SATURATED FAT: 6G; CHOLESTEROL: 46MG; SODIUM: 80MG; CARBOHYDRATES: 15G; FIBER: 4G; PROTEIN: 26G

Baked Apple, Ham, and Cheese Sliders

SERVES 4

PREP TIME:
10 MINUTES

COOK TIME:
15 MINUTES

30-MINUTE

ONE

A melody of flavors and textures comes together in these little but mighty sandwiches—crisp apples, soft rolls, melty cheese, salty ham. It's a big party on a little bun.

Nonstick cooking spray

12 Hawaiian sweet rolls or small club rolls, sliced open

¼ pound deli ham slices

1 sweet, crisp apple, thinly sliced

¼ pound deli provolone slices

1 tablespoon unsalted butter, melted

Salt

1. Preheat the oven to 375°F. Spray a 9-by-13-inch glass baking dish with nonstick cooking spray.

2. Place the bottom halves of the rolls in the baking dish, and top with the ham, draping it on to cover the rolls. Top with the apple slices, overlapping slightly, followed by the provolone and the tops of the rolls. Brush the rolls with the butter and sprinkle with salt.

3. Bake for 10 to 15 minutes, until the cheese is melty and the sandwiches are warmed through.

4. Cool slightly before serving.

VARIATION: You can substitute sliced deli turkey for the ham. The result will be less salty and more meaty.

PER SERVING CALORIES: 412; TOTAL FAT: 23G; SATURATED FAT: 13G; CHOLESTEROL: 63MG; SODIUM: 1.023MG; CARBOHYDRATES: 27G; FIBER: 3G; PROTEIN: 25G

Sheet Pan Sausage and Peppers

This is another recipe that's absolutely perfect for those evenings when time is at a premium. Most of the time is hands-off while the dish cooks so you can supervise homework, baths, and whatever else while dinner is cooking on its own. Plus, the classic combination of juicy sausage with earthy peppers and sweet onions is wonderful comfort food.

SERVES 4

PREP TIME:
10 MINUTES

COOK TIME:
30 MINUTES

GF
GLUTEN-FREE

ONE

1 pound sweet Italian sausage links

1 medium onion, halved and thinly sliced

1 green bell pepper, thinly sliced

1 red bell pepper, thinly sliced

1 tablespoon extra-virgin olive oil

Salt

Ground black pepper

1. Preheat the oven to 425°F. Line a baking sheet with parchment paper or aluminum foil.

2. Place the sausage links at the edge of the baking sheet (on the parchment paper), and pile the onion and bell peppers in the center. Drizzle with the olive oil, and season with salt and pepper.

3. Bake for 25 to 30 minutes, stirring once or twice, until the sausage is cooked through, and serve.

PER SERVING CALORIES: 400; TOTAL FAT: 34G; SATURATED FAT: 10G; CHOLESTEROL: 82MG; SODIUM: 724 MG; CARBOHYDRATES: 6G; FIBER: 2G; PROTEIN: 18G

Oven-Roasted Breaded Pork Chops

SERVES 4

PREP TIME:
5 MINUTES

COOK TIME:
25 MINUTES

30-MINUTE

ONE

It's the breading that elevates these easy pork chops to extraordinary. These are excellent with caramelized onions. To make them, sauté one to two thinly sliced onions in olive oil with a sprinkling of salt and pepper over medium-low heat for 20 to 25 minutes. When they are browned and soft, drizzle with balsamic vinegar—not too much—and cook for a couple minutes more, until the liquid evaporates.

¼ cup seasoned breadcrumbs

2 tablespoons grated
    Parmesan cheese

½ teaspoon salt

¼ teaspoon smoked paprika

4 boneless pork chops
    (about 1½ pounds total)

1. Preheat the oven to 425°F. Line a baking sheet with parchment paper or aluminum foil. Place a metal cooking rack over the parchment paper.

2. Combine the breadcrumbs, Parmesan, salt, and paprika in a zip-top bag. Shake to combine. Add the pork chops to the bag, and shake thoroughly to coat. Place on the cooking rack. Sprinkle an extra pinch of breadcrumb mixture onto each pork chop.

3. Roast for 20 to 25 minutes, until cooked through, and serve.

MAKE IT EASIER: The cooking rack helps the pork chops have a crisper coating. But if you don't have one, they can be cooked directly on the baking sheet.

PER SERVING CALORIES: 247; TOTAL FAT: 8G; SATURATED FAT: 3G; CHOLESTEROL: 84MG; SODIUM: 763MG; CARBOHYDRATES: 5G; FIBER: 0G; PROTEIN: 38G

Garlic-Ginger Pork Stir-Fry

With a flavor reminiscent of that takeout staple beef with broccoli, this stir-fry is hearty enough to be eaten alone. But it is also lovely served with rice, rice noodles, or even pasta.

SERVES 4

PREP TIME:
10 MINUTES

COOK TIME:
10 MINUTES

30-MINUTE

GLUTEN-FREE

ONE

2 tablespoons extra-virgin olive oil

1 tablespoon freshly grated ginger

4 garlic cloves, minced

1 pound boneless pork cutlets, cut into thin strips

2 cups fresh broccoli, chopped

2 tablespoons soy sauce or tamari (gluten-free, if needed)

1. In a large skillet over medium heat, heat the olive oil. Add the ginger and garlic and cook, stirring, until fragrant, about 1 minute. Add the pork and broccoli and cook, stirring occasionally, for 5 to 7 minutes, until there isn't any visible pink remaining on the pork.

2. Drizzle with the soy sauce. Cook for an additional 3 to 4 minutes, until the broccoli is crisp-tender and the amount of liquid in the pan is reduced by about half, and serve.

VARIATION: You can substitute green beans for the broccoli. Chop them into bite-size pieces before adding to the skillet.

PER SERVING CALORIES: 225; TOTAL FAT: 12G; SATURATED FAT: 3G; CHOLESTEROL: 54MG; SODIUM: 775MG; CARBOHYDRATES: 5G; FIBER: 1G; PROTEIN: 27G

Rosemary-Garlic Pork Tenderloin

SERVES 6

PREP TIME:
10 MINUTES

COOK TIME:
35 MINUTES,
PLUS 15 MINUTES
TO REST

GF
GLUTEN-FREE

ONE

Earthy rosemary and piquant garlic load this pork tenderloin with flavor. It's great served with mashed potatoes. This is a fantastic recipe for special occasions or when company's coming.

1 boneless pork tenderloin
   (1⅓ to 1½ pounds total)
2 garlic cloves, thinly sliced

1 teaspoon salt
1 teaspoon dried rosemary
¼ teaspoon ground black pepper

1. Preheat the oven to 425°F. The oven rack should be in the center of the oven. Place a nonstick baking sheet in the oven while it's preheating.

2. On a cutting board, cut the tenderloin halfway through into 6 slices of roughly equal thickness. Press the garlic slices into the cuts.

3. In a small mixing bowl, stir together the salt, rosemary, and pepper. Rub all over the tenderloin, including into the cuts.

4. Place the tenderloin on the hot pan and roast for 30 to 35 minutes.

5. Remove the tenderloin from the oven and let it sit for 15 minutes. Slice into thin slices and serve.

PER SERVING CALORIES: 137; TOTAL FAT: 4G; SATURATED FAT: 1G; CHOLESTEROL: 74MG; SODIUM: 447MG; CARBOHYDRATES: 0G; FIBER: 0G; PROTEIN: 23G

Slow Cooker Barbecue Pulled Pork

The rich sauce makes this pulled pork divine. Enjoy leftovers in sandwiches or on top of a mound of mashed potatoes. Try serving this in a wrap with Cheddar cheese and caramelized onions, too. Pulled pork leftovers are delightful piled on macaroni and cheese.

SERVES 6

PREP TIME:
10 MINUTES

COOK TIME:
10 HOURS

FREEZER-
FRIENDLY

GF
GLUTEN-FREE

ONE

2 to 3 pounds boneless pork loin

1 (6-ounce) can tomato paste

⅓ cup water

¼ cup brown sugar

2 tablespoons molasses

1 to 1½ teaspoons salt

½ teaspoon ground black pepper

1. Place the pork loin in the slow cooker.

2. In a medium mixing bowl, whisk together the tomato paste, water, brown sugar, molasses, salt, and pepper. Taste and adjust seasoning. Pour over the pork.

3. Cover the slow cooker and cook on low for 8 to 10 hours, until the pork is fall-apart tender.

4. Use two forks to shred the pork in the slow cooker, stir the shreds into the sauce, and serve.

5. Store leftovers in the refridgerator for up to 5 days or freeze in an airtight container or zip-top freezer bag for up to 4 months. To reheat, defrost completely and microwave for 2 to 3 minutes on high, until heated throughout.

PER SERVING CALORIES: 258; TOTAL FAT: 5G; SATURATED FAT: 2G; CHOLESTEROL: 98MG; SODIUM: 499MG; CARBOHYDRATES: 19G; FIBER: 1G; PROTEIN: 32G

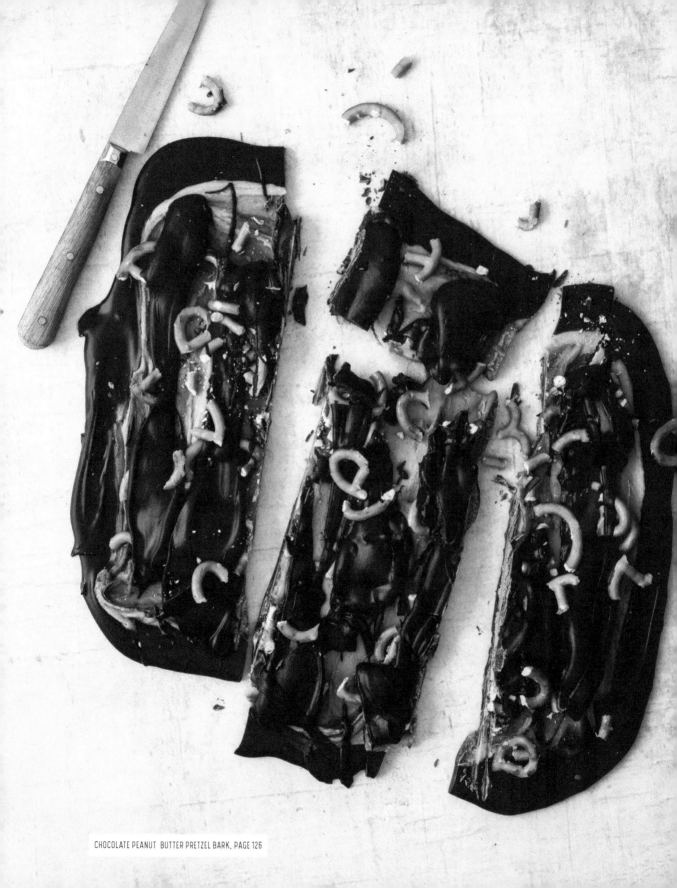

CHOCOLATE PEANUT BUTTER PRETZEL BARK, PAGE 126

8

DESSERTS AND SWEET TREATS

Peanut Butter and Banana Milkshake

**MAKES
1 MILKSHAKE**

PREP TIME:
5 MINUTES

This is the milkshake you've been looking for. It's creamy, smooth, and filled with the oh-so-good combination of peanut butter and banana.

30-MINUTE

**GF
GLUTEN-FREE**

NO-COOK

ONE

VEGETARIAN

⅓ cup milk

1 banana, broken into chunks

1 cup vanilla ice cream

1 tablespoon peanut butter

1. In a blender, combine the milk, banana, ice cream, and peanut butter, and blend until smooth.

2. Pour into a glass and enjoy immediately.

VARIATION: For an even frostier drink, freeze the banana first. Peel it, then break it into pieces and store in a zip-top freezer bag or plastic container in the freezer. Just add the frozen pieces to the blender.

PER SERVING CALORIES: 483; TOTAL FAT: 18G; SATURATED FAT: 8G; CHOLESTEROL: 80MG; SODIUM: 209MG; CARBOHYDRATES: 70G; FIBER: 4G; PROTEIN: 14G

Easy Strawberry Froyo

Creamy, fruity, and refreshing, this recipe for easy homemade soft-serve takes mere minutes to make. This also works as a great base recipe for froyo, as you can add or sub other frozen fruits, such as peaches, raspberries, or bananas.

SERVES 4

PREP TIME:
5 MINUTES

30-MINUTE

FREEZER-
FRIENDLY

GLUTEN-FREE

NO-COOK

ONE

1 cup vanilla Greek yogurt

1 (12-ounce) package frozen strawberries (or 12 ounces any frozen fruit)

2 tablespoons honey

1. In a blender, combine the yogurt, strawberries, and honey. Blend on high until smooth, stopping and pushing down the berries to help them blend as needed.

2. Divide among four bowls and enjoy immediately.

3. Can't finish it all? Store leftovers in an airtight container in the freezer and enjoy as desired. (Do not defrost—it's frozen yogurt!)

VEGETARIAN

VARIATION: For Strawberry Banana Froyo, substitute 1 banana for the honey. (It will be sufficiently sweet!)

PER SERVING CALORIES: 99; TOTAL FAT: 2G; SATURATED FAT: 1G; CHOLESTEROL: 8MG; SODIUM: 30MG; CARBOHYDRATES: 19G; FIBER: 2G; PROTEIN: 3G

Raspberry Yogurt Fool

SERVES 6

PREP TIME:
20 MINUTES,
PLUS 1 HOUR TO
CHILL

GF
GLUTEN-FREE

NO-COOK

VEGETARIAN

This isn't a mousse—it doesn't hold a shape like that. It's not a pudding either—it's too light and airy for that. A fool is somewhere between these two desserts; it's refreshing without being heavy or overtly sweet. Best of all, it really celebrates the flavor of the fruit. Strawberries would also work well here.

2 cups raspberries

½ cup powdered (confectioners') sugar

1¼ cup vanilla Greek yogurt

2 egg whites

1. In a food processor, process the raspberries and powdered sugar until smooth—about 30 seconds.

2. In a large mixing bowl, stir together the raspberry mixture and yogurt until smooth.

3. In a medium mixing bowl, whisk the egg whites until stiff—about 10 minutes.

4. Add the egg whites to the raspberries, and fold together until fully combined.

5. Spoon the raspberry mixture into serving glasses or bowls, and chill for at least one hour before serving.

MAKE IT EASIER: Rather than all that whisking, use a blender or an electric hand mixer to beat the egg whites. It will be quicker and easier.

PER SERVING CALORIES: 90; TOTAL FAT: 2G; SATURATED FAT: 1G; CHOLESTEROL: 7MG; SODIUM: 42MG; CARBOHYDRATES: 16G; FIBER: 3G; PROTEIN: 3G

Strawberries and Cream Parfait

Sweet, macerated strawberries and lightly sweetened whipped cream combine for a light, simple, layered dessert. Serve this dessert in clear parfait glasses for the prettiest (and most impressive) presentation.

SERVES 4

PREP TIME:
15 MINUTES

30-MINUTE

GF
GLUTEN-FREE

NO-COOK

VEGETARIAN

2 cups strawberries, quartered

1 tablespoon sugar

1 cup heavy (whipping) cream

2 tablespoons powdered (confectioners') sugar

½ teaspoon pure vanilla extract

4 graham cracker squares (optional, gluten-free if needed)

1. In a small mixing bowl, stir together the strawberries and sugar. Let sit while you make the whipped cream.

2. In a large mixing bowl (or the bowl of a stand mixer), combine the heavy cream, powdered sugar, and vanilla extract. Beat with a whisk, electric hand mixer, or stand mixer until stiff peaks form.

3. Spoon a layer of strawberries into four serving glasses, then a layer of whipped cream, then strawberries, then whipped cream again. If desired, crumble the graham crackers on top.

MAKE IT EASIER: You can substitute refrigerated whipped cream for homemade, but make sure it's made with real cream for the best flavor.

PER SERVING CALORIES: 258; TOTAL FAT: 22G; SATURATED FAT: 14G; CHOLESTEROL: 82MG; SODIUM: 23MG; CARBOHYDRATES: 15G; FIBER: 2G; PROTEIN: 2G

Birthday Cake Mug Cake

SERVES 1

PREP TIME:
5 MINUTES

COOK TIME:
2 MINUTES

(30)

30-MINUTE

ONE

VEGETARIAN

Tender cake in about a minute? Yep, it's possible. This sweet confetti cake is perfect for celebrating all kinds of things—including birthdays. Eat it with a spoon right from the mug.

3 tablespoons all-purpose flour

¼ teaspoon baking powder

1 tablespoon sugar

2 tablespoons milk

1 tablespoon vegetable oil

½ teaspoon sprinkles

1. In a ramekin or an 8-ounce mug, stir together the flour, baking powder, sugar, milk, and oil until well combined and smooth. Stir in the sprinkles.

2. Microwave on high for 1 to 1½ minutes, until cooked through.

3. Remove from the microwave. Enjoy right away.

VARIATION: Sprinkle a few chocolate chips on top before cooking. When it comes out of the microwave, spread the melted chocolate around with the back of a spoon for instant frosting.

PER SERVING CALORIES: 271; TOTAL FAT: 15G; SATURATED FAT: 2G; CHOLESTEROL: 3MG; SODIUM: 102MG; CARBOHYDRATES: 32G; FIBER: 1G; PROTEIN: 3G

Vanilla Pudding

Creamy, sweet vanilla pudding is such a treat. I love to pack this pudding in individual containers to put in my kids' lunch boxes on weekdays.

SERVES 4

PREP TIME:
5 MINUTES

COOK TIME:
15 MINUTES, PLUS
1 HOUR TO CHILL

⅓ cup granulated sugar

2 tablespoons cornstarch

1½ cups milk

2 teaspoons pure vanilla extract

GF
GLUTEN-FREE

ONE

VEGETARIAN

1. In a medium saucepan with the heat off, stir together the sugar, cornstarch, milk, and vanilla extract. Turn the heat on to medium and cook, stirring constantly, until boiling. Reduce the heat to low and cook for 1 to 2 minutes, stirring constantly. The pudding is done when it's thickened and is a uniform color. Remove from the heat.

2. Transfer the pudding to a bowl and chill in the refrigerator for at least 1 hour before serving.

VARIATION: You can substitute vanilla bean seeds for the vanilla extract. Use the seeds from 1 to 2 vanilla beans.

PER SERVING CALORIES: 140; TOTAL FAT: 3G; SATURATED FAT: 2G; CHOLESTEROL: 9MG; SODIUM: 37MG; CARBOHYDRATES: 25G; FIBER: 0G; PROTEIN: 3G

Peanut Butter Pudding

SERVES 4

PREP TIME:
5 MINUTES

COOK TIME:
15 MINUTES, PLUS
1 HOUR TO CHILL

GF
GLUTEN-FREE

ONE

VEGETARIAN

For all you peanut butter lovers, this pudding is heavenly. I like it best served with crumbled graham crackers on top—a simple take on peanut butter pie. But if gluten is a concern for you, try some chopped honey-roasted peanuts on top.

¼ cup granulated sugar

¼ cup peanut butter

2 tablespoons cornstarch

1½ cups milk

Crumbled graham crackers (optional)

1. In a medium saucepan with the heat off, stir together the sugar, peanut butter, cornstarch, and milk. Turn on the heat to medium and cook, stirring constantly, until boiling. Reduce the heat to low and cook for 1 to 2 minutes, stirring constantly. The pudding is done when it's thickened and is a uniform color. Remove from the heat.

2. Transfer the pudding to a bowl and chill in the refrigerator for at least 1 hour before serving. Top with graham crackers, if desired.

VARIATION: You can substitute other nut butters, such as almond or cashew butter, for the peanut butter. Top with graham crackers, if desired.

PER SERVING CALORIES: 213; TOTAL FAT: 11G; SATURATED FAT: 3G; CHOLESTEROL: 9MG; SODIUM: 114MG; CARBOHYDRATES: 25G; FIBER: 1G; PROTEIN: 6G

Easy Oven S'mores

These s'mores are just like the ones you make over the campfire in the summertime, but they are so easy to make indoors in the oven. Vegan graham crackers and chocolate are easy to find in the supermarket. Who wants an ooey-gooey bite?

MAKES 1

PREP TIME:
5 MINUTES

COOK TIME:
5 MINUTES

2 squares graham crackers

1 square chocolate

1 marshmallow, halved

1. On a baking sheet, place one graham cracker. Top with one chocolate square and the two marshmallow halves.

2. Place the baking sheet under the broiler. Broil for 2 to 3 minutes, until the marshmallow is browned.

3. Remove from the oven, top with second graham cracker, and enjoy.

30-MINUTE

ONE

VEGAN

VARIATION: You can use other chocolate-based candies instead of the chocolate square, such as miniature peanut butter cups or peppermint patties.

PER SERVING CALORIES: 243; TOTAL FAT: 12G; SATURATED FAT: 6G; CHOLESTEROL: 2MG; SODIUM: 93MG; CARBOHYDRATES: 31G; FIBER: 3G; PROTEIN: 3G

Crispy S'mores Marshmallow Treats

**MAKES
12 SQUARES**

PREP TIME:
5 MINUTES

COOK TIME:
15 MINUTES

30-MINUTE

VEGETARIAN

When I was a little girl, my mom and I would make marshmallow treats from time to time. The sticky, gooey mess of butter, marshmallows, and crispy cereal transformed into these ooey-gooey bars I adored. I still do. This dessert treat combines those with another childhood favorite: s'mores. It's nostalgic and delicious and all those good things.

¼ cup unsalted butter

1 (10-ounce) bag marshmallows

6 cups crisped rice cereal

Nonstick cooking spray

1 cup milk chocolate chips

1 cup crumbled graham crackers

1. In a medium saucepan over medium heat, melt the butter. Add the marshmallows and cook, stirring constantly, until melted.

2. Remove from the heat and immediately begin adding the cereal a little at a time, stirring constantly until it's all incorporated.

3. Spray a 9-by-13-inch glass baking dish with nonstick cooking spray. Pour the mixture into the prepared dish, and press down evenly.

4. Immediately, while the mixture is still hot, spread the chocolate chips and the graham crackers all over the marshmallow cereal mixture. Let sit for a few minutes, then gently press the graham crackers down into the melted chocolate.

5. Let cool and harden completely before cutting into 12 squares and serving.

~~~~~~

VARIATION: You can substitute 1 cup of chopped milk or dark chocolate for the milk chocolate chips.

PER SERVING (1 SQUARE) CALORIES: 245; TOTAL FAT: 8G; SATURATED FAT: 5G; CHOLESTEROL: 11MG; SODIUM: 216MG; CARBOHYDRATES: 41G; FIBER: 1G; PROTEIN: 2G

Chocolate and Peanut Butter Pretzel Bark

SERVES 8

PREP TIME:
10 MINUTES

COOK TIME:
5 MINUTES,
PLUS AT LEAST
30 MINUTES TO
CHILL

GF
GLUTEN-FREE

VEGETARIAN

I'm the kind of girl who eats peanut butter from the jar. That's how much I love sweet, creamy peanut spread. In this candy, it costars with rich chocolate and salty pretzels—what more could you ask for in a dessert?

½ cup peanut butter

¼ cup powdered (confectioners') sugar

2 teaspoons unsalted butter, softened

½ cup broken-up salted pretzels (gluten-free, if needed)

2 cups dark chocolate chips

1. In a small mixing bowl, stir together the peanut butter, powdered sugar, and butter until smooth.

2. Melt the dark chocolate (see the Make It Easier tip).

3. Place wax paper on a baking sheet. Spread half the melted chocolate on the baking sheet. Top with the peanut butter–pretzel mixture, followed by the other half of the chocolate.

4. Chill in the refrigerator. Allow to harden completely before cutting into pieces and serving.

MAKE IT EASIER: There are two ways to melt chocolate. Place the chocolate chips in a glass microwave-safe bowl and cook for 30 seconds, stir, and repeat until smooth. Or place them in a metal mixing bowl set on top of a small saucepan with water in the bottom (don't let the water touch the bowl). Heat the water to a simmer with the chocolate chips in the mixing bowl, stirring constantly, until smooth.

PER SERVING CALORIES: 400; TOTAL FAT: 26G; SATURATED FAT: 12G; CHOLESTEROL: 5MG; SODIUM: 109MG; CARBOHYDRATES: 37G; FIBER: 5G; PROTEIN: 7G

Double Chocolate Palmiers

**MAKES
20 COOKIES**

PREP TIME:
10 MINUTES

COOK TIME:
20 MINUTES

30-MINUTE

ONE

VEGETARIAN

Crispy and filled with chocolate, these are sometimes called elephant's ears. Whatever you call these easy cookies, just know that they are g-o-o-d good!

1 sheet frozen puff pastry, defrosted

⅓ cup chocolate hazelnut spread

¼ cup chocolate chips

1. Preheat the oven to 400°F. Line a baking sheet with aluminum foil.

2. Lay the puff pastry on a cutting board. Spread one half with chocolate hazelnut spread, and sprinkle with the chocolate chips. Roll each side toward the center until the dough meets in the middle.

3. Cut into ¼-inch slices. Place the slices on the prepared baking sheet, leaving 1 inch between each piece.

4. Bake for 15 to 18 minutes, until golden. Cool before enjoying.

VARIATION: You can use any type of chocolate chips here. Sprinkle with coarse sugar before baking, for an added sweet crunch.

PER SERVING (1 COOKIE) CALORIES: 108; TOTAL FAT: 7G; SATURATED FAT: 3G; CHOLESTEROL: 0MG; SODIUM: 31MG; CARBOHYDRATES: 10G; FIBER: 1G; PROTEIN: 1G

Blackberry-Apple Crisp

Blackberries have big flavor. And in this crisp, they star. This dessert is lovely with a scoop of vanilla ice cream. If gluten is an issue for you, be sure to look for gluten-free oats.

SERVES 6

PREP TIME:
10 MINUTES

COOK TIME:
55 MINUTES

GF
GLUTEN-FREE

ONE

VEGETARIAN

Nonstick cooking spray

2 apples, diced

2 cups blackberries

⅓ cup light brown sugar, plus 1 tablespoon, divided

⅓ cup uncooked rolled oats

5 tablespoons unsalted butter, melted

1. Preheat the oven to 375°F. Spray an 8-by-8-inch glass baking dish with nonstick cooking spray.

2. In a medium mixing bowl, stir together the apples, blackberries, and 1 tablespoon of light brown sugar. Spread evenly in the glass baking dish.

3. In a small mixing bowl, stir the remaining ⅓ cup of light brown sugar together with the oats and melted butter. Sprinkle evenly over the fruit mixture.

4. Bake for 45 to 55 minutes, until the top is golden and the fruit is bubbling at the sides. Remove from the oven and let cool slightly before serving.

VARIATION: For added zing, stir 1 tablespoon of freshly grated ginger into the fruit mixture before spreading it in the baking dish.

PER SERVING CALORIES: 229; TOTAL FAT: 10G; SATURATED FAT: 6G; CHOLESTEROL: 25MG; SODIUM: 73MG; CARBOHYDRATES: 34G; FIBER: 5G; PROTEIN: 2G

Warm Pear Crumble

SERVES 6

PREP TIME:
10 MINUTES

COOK TIME:
55 MINUTES

GF
GLUTEN-FREE

ONE

VEGETARIAN

For this dessert, the tender, mild pears are topped with a sweet, cookie-like crumble. For added zing, add 1 teaspoon of freshly grated ginger to the pears before baking.

Nonstick cooking spray

4 pears, cored and thinly sliced

¼ cup sugar, plus
1 tablespoon, divided

¼ cup all-purpose flour, plus
2 tablespoons, divided

¼ cup uncooked rolled oats
(use gluten-free if you have a
gluten sensitivity)

¼ cup cold unsalted butter, cut
into pieces

1. Preheat the oven to 375°F. Spray an 8-by-8-inch glass baking dish with nonstick cooking spray.

2. In a medium mixing bowl, toss together the pears with 1 tablespoon of sugar and 2 tablespoons of flour. Spread evenly in the glass baking dish.

3. In a small mixing bowl, stir together the remaining ¼ cup of sugar with the remaining ¼ cup of flour and the oats. Add the butter and cut into the mixture using two butter knives. The mixture should resemble coarse crumbs. Sprinkle evenly over the pears.

4. Bake for 45 to 55 minutes, until the crumble is golden and bubbling at the sides. Remove from the oven and cool before serving.

MAKE IT EASIER: To cut in the butter, pull two butter knives through the mixture in opposite directions close to each other, cutting the butter into smaller and smaller pieces.

PER SERVING CALORIES: 218; TOTAL FAT: 8G; SATURATED FAT: 5G; CHOLESTEROL: 20MG; SODIUM: 55MG; CARBOHYDRATES: 36G; FIBER: 4G; PROTEIN: 2G

Mini Blueberry Pies

These little pies have a wonderful blueberry flavor. They're perfect for serving at dinner parties—and for packing in lunch boxes. Although wild blueberries aren't always available fresh, you can often find them in the freezer section. If they're not available, though, any blueberries will do.

MAKES 12 MINI PIES

PREP TIME:
15 MINUTES

COOK TIME:
20 MINUTES

ONE

VEGETARIAN

1 refrigerated piecrust

1½ cups wild blueberries

2 tablespoons brown sugar

2 teaspoons cornstarch

1 teaspoon ground cinnamon

1. Preheat the oven to 425°F. Line the cups of a 12-muffin pan with paper liners.

2. Roll out the piecrust on a cutting board, and use a large cookie or biscuit cutter (or a glass) to cut out 12 rounds. Gather and roll the excess dough as needed to cut the last few. Press the rounds into the lined muffin cups.

3. In a small mixing bowl, stir together the blueberries, brown sugar, cornstarch, and cinnamon. Divide evenly among the piecrust rounds.

4. Bake for 18 to 20 minutes, until the crusts are golden and the blueberry filling is bubbly.

5. Cool completely before serving.

VARIATION: Try serving a warm pie with a scoop of ice cream for each guest.

PER SERVING (1 PIE) CALORIES: 107; TOTAL FAT: 5G; SATURATED FAT: 2G; CHOLESTEROL: OMG; SODIUM: 79MG; CARBOHYDRATES: 15G; FIBER: 1G; PROTEIN: 1G

Apple-Strawberry Turnovers

**MAKES
4 TURNOVERS**

PREP TIME:
10 MINUTES

COOK TIME:
30 MINUTES

ONE

VEGETARIAN

The crisp, flaky crust hides a sweet berry-apple filling in this dessert. You can substitute raspberries for the strawberries, if you prefer. These are best served warm.

1 sheet frozen puff pastry, thawed

1 cup chopped fresh strawberries

1 apple, diced

2 tablespoons sugar, plus extra for dusting

1 teaspoon unsalted butter, melted

1. Preheat the oven to 400°F. Line a baking sheet with parchment paper.

2. Dust a cutting board with flour. Lay the puff pastry on the board and roll it out to a square about 15-by-15 inches. Cut that into four squares.

3. In a medium mixing bowl, stir together the strawberries, apple, and 2 tablespoons of sugar. Divide the fruit mixture evenly among the four puff pastry squares, making a mound in the middle. Using a fingertip dipped in water, moisten the edges of each puff pastry square. Fold over to form a triangle, and press the edges closed.

4. Transfer the turnovers to the baking sheet. Brush each with the butter, then dust with a pinch of sugar. Use a sharp knife to cut two slits into each turnover.

5. Bake for 25 to 30 minutes, until golden brown, and cool slightly before serving.

~~~~~~

MAKE IT EASIER: You can find parchment paper in the grocery store near the plastic wraps, aluminum foil, and wax paper. It's a disposable paper used to line pans to give them a nonstick surface. It also tempers the heat of the baking sheet, so the dough won't burn as easily.

PER SERVING (1 TURNOVER) CALORIES: 379; TOTAL FAT: 23G; SATURATED FAT: 9G; CHOLESTEROL: 3MG; SODIUM: 149MG; CARBOHYDRATES: 41G; FIBER: 3G; PROTEIN: 5G

EASY PICKLED CARROTS, PAGE 141

9

DRESSINGS, SAUCES, AND STAPLES

Lemon-Thyme Vinaigrette

MAKES ABOUT
½ CUP

PREP TIME:
5 MINUTES

30-MINUTE

GF
GLUTEN-FREE

NO-COOK

ONE

VEGAN

If I had to pick just one herb to cook with, it would probably be thyme because it's so versatile and the pleasant flavor adds to so many dishes. This tart, refreshing vinaigrette made with thyme is perfect drizzled on salads, steamed asparagus, and other veggies.

Juice of 1 lemon (about ¼ cup)

¼ cup extra-virgin olive oil

½ teaspoon dried thyme

⅛ teaspoon dry ground mustard

½ teaspoon salt

1. In a small mixing bowl, whisk together the lemon juice, olive oil, thyme, mustard, and salt thoroughly until combined.

2. Store in an airtight container in the refrigerator for up to 5 days.

VARIATION: For an earthier version of this dressing, use dried rosemary instead of thyme.

PER SERVING (2 TABLESPOONS) CALORIES: 124; TOTAL FAT: 14G; SATURATED FAT: 2G; CHOLESTEROL: 0MG; SODIUM: 291MG; CARBOHYDRATES: 1G; FIBER: 0G; PROTEIN: 0G

Honey-Balsamic Vinaigrette

Tangy and slightly sweet, this vinaigrette is great on salads of all kinds. Be sure to taste your balsamic vinegar before making the dressing, though. If it tastes sweet on its own, reduce the honey to 1 tablespoon.

MAKES ALMOST 1 CUP

PREP TIME: 5 MINUTES

⅓ cup balsamic vinegar

2 tablespoons honey

1 teaspoon Dijon mustard

½ cup extra-virgin olive oil

Salt

1. In a small mixing bowl, whisk together the balsamic vinegar, honey, and mustard until well combined.

2. Add the olive oil in a steady stream, whisking constantly, until fully combined. Season with salt, and whisk again.

3. Store in an airtight container in the refrigerator for up to 1 week.

30-MINUTE

GF
GLUTEN-FREE

NO-COOK

ONE

VEGETARIAN

VARIATION: This dressing is lovely on its own, but for more dimension, try whisking in one clove of finely minced garlic in step 1. You can also make it vegan by subbing in agave or maple syrup for the honey.

PER SERVING (2 TABLESPOONS) CALORIES: 129; TOTAL FAT: 14G; SATURATED FAT: 2G; CHOLESTEROL: 2MG; SODIUM: 0MG; CARBOHYDRATES: 2G; FIBER: 0G; PROTEIN: 0G

Creamy Avocado-Cilantro Vinaigrette

MAKES ABOUT 1½ CUPS

PREP TIME: 10 MINUTES

30-MINUTE

GF
GLUTEN-FREE

NO-COOK

ONE

V
VEGAN

Lime gives this vinaigrette a pleasant tartness, while the avocado provides the creaminess. Try this vinaigrette on rice bowls, salads, or to dress your favorite wrap. Because of the avocado, you should eat it within a few days of making it.

1 ripe avocado, pitted and peeled

Juice of 1 lime (about ¼ cup)

1 tablespoon chopped fresh cilantro

¼ cup extra-virgin olive oil

½ cup water

Salt

Ground black pepper

1. In a blender, combine the avocado, lime juice, and cilantro. Blend until smooth. With the blender running on low, add the olive oil in a steady stream, followed by the water.

2. Taste, and season with salt and pepper.

3. Store in an airtight container in the refridgerator. Use within a day or two.

VARIATION: Not a cilantro fan? You can substitute fresh basil. It will give the vinaigrette a more savory brightness.

PER SERVING (2 TABLESPOONS) CALORIES: 60; TOTAL FAT: 6G; SATURATED FAT: 1G; CHOLESTEROL: 0MG; SODIUM: 5MG; CARBOHYDRATES: 1G; FIBER: 1G; PROTEIN: 0G

Spicy Pineapple Salsa

This salsa embraces the idea of "sweet and spicy." Make no mistake, though—it has bite. This salsa is great served with chips for dipping, but it's also delicious with quesadillas and tacos. Also try it with grilled chicken.

MAKES ABOUT 2 CUPS

PREP TIME: 10 MINUTES

30-MINUTE

FREEZER-FRIENDLY

GF

GLUTEN-FREE

NO-COOK

ONE

(V)

VEGAN

1 (8-ounce) can crushed pineapple, drained

¼ cup diced red bell peppers

1 jalapeño pepper, finely chopped

1 teaspoon minced fresh cilantro

Salt

1. In a medium mixing bowl, stir together the pineapple, bell peppers, jalapeño pepper, and cilantro, and season with salt.

2. Let sit for at least 5 minutes before using to allow the flavors to blend.

3. To freeze, store in a freezer-friendly container in the freezer for up to 4 months. Defrost in the refrigerator overnight and use as desired.

PER SERVING (¼ CUP) CALORIES: 19; TOTAL FAT: 0G; SATURATED FAT: 0G; CHOLESTEROL: 0MG; SODIUM: 7MG; CARBOHYDRATES: 5G; FIBER: 1G; PROTEIN: 0G

Chunky Tomato Salsa

**MAKES ABOUT
3 CUPS**

PREP TIME:
10 MINUTES

30-MINUTE

**FREEZER-
FRIENDLY**

**GF
GLUTEN-FREE**

NO-COOK

VEGAN

Fresh and flavorful, this salsa is great on grilled fish (swordfish is a favorite of mine) or chicken. It can also be delightful spooned onto Cheddar omelets. Make it milder by removing the seeds from the jalapeño pepper. Want it hotter? Add a second pepper.

3 cups diced tomatoes

¾ cup diced red onion

1 jalapeño pepper, chopped

1 garlic clove, minced

2 tablespoons finely chopped
   fresh cilantro

Salt

Ground black pepper

Tortilla chips, for serving

1. In a large mixing bowl, stir together the tomatoes, onion, jalapeño pepper, garlic, and cilantro, and season with salt and pepper.

2. Transfer half of the salsa to a food processor, and pulse until it is a uniform consistency. Return the mixture to the bowl and stir well.

3. Serve with tortilla chips.

4. This makes a big batch, but it also freezes well. Transfer leftovers to a freezer-safe container and freeze. Thaw overnight in the refrigerator before serving.

VARIATION: Want to add even more flavor to this salsa? Stir in the juice of 1 lime.

PER SERVING (¼ CUP) CALORIES: 13; TOTAL FAT: 0G; SATURATED FAT: 0G; CHOLESTEROL: 0MG; SODIUM: 7MG; CARBOHYDRATES: 3G; FIBER: 1G; PROTEIN: 1G

Easy Pickled Carrots

With a fresh, bright flavor, these pickled carrots add a nice zing to so many dishes. Use them to top rice bowls or chicken breasts, toss them in salads, brighten up a plain vegetable dish, or throw them in wraps with some sliced deli meat. Elevate your basic ramen noodles by adding some of these on top. Yum!

MAKES 2 CUPS

PREP TIME:
5 MINUTES, PLUS
20 MINUTES TO
CHILL

2 cups julienne-cut carrots

2 tablespoons seasoned rice vinegar

1 teaspoon grated fresh ginger

Salt

1. In a 2-cup container with a tight-fitting lid, combine the carrots, vinegar, and ginger, and season with salt. Stir or shake well to combine.

2. Chill in the refrigerator for at least 20 minutes before using.

3. Store in the refrigerator for up to 1 week.

30-MINUTE

GF
GLUTEN-FREE

NO-COOK

ONE

(V)
VEGAN

MAKE IT EASIER: Julienned carrots are available precut in many supermarkets, making this even easier to whip up.

PER SERVING (½ CUP) CALORIES: 28; TOTAL FAT: 0G; SATURATED FAT: 0G; CHOLESTEROL: 0MG; SODIUM: 57MG; CARBOHYDRATES: 6G; FIBER: 2G; PROTEIN: 1G

Classic Basil Pesto

**MAKES ABOUT
1 CUP**

PREP TIME:
10 MINUTES

30-MINUTE

FREEZER-
FRIENDLY

GF

GLUTEN-FREE

NO-COOK

ONE

VEGETARIAN

This is one of those recipes that demands the best ingredients for the best results. The higher-quality cheese and olive oil you use, the more robust the flavor will be. Likewise, the freshest basil will give this pesto the best taste.

2 cups packed basil leaves

1 garlic clove

⅓ cup pine nuts

⅓ cup grated Parmesan cheese

½ cup extra-virgin olive oil

Salt

1. In the food processor, combine the basil, garlic, pine nuts, and Parmesan. Pulse until evenly chopped.

2. With the food processor running on low, add the oil in a steady stream through the chute until combined. Taste and season with salt.

3. Store in an airtight container in the refrigerator for up to 1 week. To freeze, store in a freezer-friendly container in the freezer for up to 4 months. Defrost in the refrigerator overnight, and use as desired.

VARIATION: All kinds of hard cheeses, such as Romano, are excellent in this pesto.

PER SERVING (1 TABLESPOON) CALORIES: 88; TOTAL FAT: 9G; SATURATED FAT: 1G; CHOLESTEROL: 2MG; SODIUM: 35MG; CARBOHYDRATES: 1G; FIBER: 0G; PROTEIN: 1G

Easy Tomato Marinara

Homemade marinara sauce is so simple to whip up—it's almost as easy as buying it. And when you make your own, you get to fully control what goes into it and how it tastes. Try this sauce on pasta or chicken and in vegetable bakes.

MAKES 3 CUPS

PREP TIME:
5 MINUTES

COOK TIME:
20 MINUTES

30-MINUTE

FREEZER-FRIENDLY

GF

GLUTEN-FREE

ONE

V

VEGAN

1 tablespoon extra-virgin olive oil

1 small yellow onion, diced

2 garlic cloves, minced

1 (28-ounce) can puréed tomatoes

1 tablespoon chopped fresh basil

Salt

Ground black pepper

1. In a medium saucepan over medium heat, heat the olive oil. Add the onion and cook, stirring occasionally, until browned, 5 to 7 minutes.

2. Add the garlic and stir for 30 seconds, or until fragrant.

3. Stir in the tomatoes and basil. Cover, reduce the heat to low, and simmer for 15 minutes. Taste, and season with salt and pepper.

4. To freeze, store in a freezer-friendly container in the freezer for up to 4 months. Defrost in the refrigerator overnight and use as desired.

VARIATION: Try adding more herbs, such as fresh or dried oregano and thyme, to this recipe for a more robust flavor.

PER SERVING (½ CUP) CALORIES: 58; TOTAL FAT: 2G; SATURATED FAT: 0G; CHOLESTEROL: 0MG; SODIUM: 181MG; CARBOHYDRATES: 11G; FIBER: 3G; PROTEIN: 2G

Mixed-Berry Refrigerator Jam

MAKES ABOUT 1 CUP

PREP TIME: 5 MINUTES

COOK TIME: 30 MINUTES

FREEZER-FRIENDLY

GF
GLUTEN-FREE

ONE

(V)
VEGAN

The bright berry flavor of this jam makes it perfect to enjoy on bread, biscuits, ice cream, and yogurt. It's also lovely swirled into oatmeal.

2 cups frozen mixed berries

½ cup granulated sugar

1 teaspoon grated lemon zest

1. In a medium saucepan over medium-high heat, combine the berries, sugar, and lemon zest. Stir well. Bring to a boil, stirring constantly.

2. Reduce the heat to low and simmer for 15 to 20 minutes, or until the jam is thickened and seems to move as one. Stir frequently as it cooks.

3. Transfer the jam to a glass container with a tight-fitting lid and cool completely. Cover and store in the refrigerator for up to 2 weeks.

4. To freeze, store in a freezer-friendly container in the freezer for up to 6 months. Defrost in the refrigerator overnight and use as desired.

MAKE IT EASIER: Save old jam jars and reuse them for recipes like this. They are perfect for storing homemade jam in the refrigerator.

PER SERVING (1 TABLESPOON) CALORIES: 34; TOTAL FAT: 0G; SATURATED FAT: 0G; CHOLESTEROL: 0MG; SODIUM: 1MG; CARBOHYDRATES: 9G; FIBER: 1G; PROTEIN: 0G

Easy Homemade Biscuits

These biscuits are as simple as they come—just stir, splat, and bake. But they are also so satisfying.

MAKES
12 BISCUITS

PREP TIME:
5 MINUTES

COOK TIME:
25 MINUTES

2 cups self-rising flour

1 cup club soda

1 tablespoon unsalted butter, melted

1 teaspoon honey

½ teaspoon salt

30-MINUTE

ONE

VEGETARIAN

1. Preheat the oven to 375°F. Line the muffin cups of a 12-cup pan with paper liners.

2. In a large mixing bowl, stir together the flour, club soda, butter, honey, and salt until well combined. Spoon into the 12 muffin cups.

3. Bake for 20 to 25 minutes, or until cooked through, and serve.

VARIATION: Enjoy these biscuits with Mixed-Berry Refrigerator Jam (page 144).

PER SERVING (1 BISCUIT) CALORIES: 84; TOTAL FAT: 1G; SATURATED FAT: 1G; CHOLESTEROL: 3MG; SODIUM: 372MG; CARBOHYDRATES: 16G; FIBER: 1G; PROTEIN: 2G

MEASUREMENT CONVERSIONS

VOLUME EQUIVALENTS (LIQUID)

STANDARD	US STANDARD (OUNCES)	METRIC (APPROXIMATE)
2 tablespoons	1 fl. oz.	30 mL
¼ cup	2 fl. oz.	60 mL
½ cup	4 fl. oz.	120 mL
1 cup	8 fl. oz.	240 mL
1½ cups	12 fl. oz.	355 mL
2 cups or 1 pint	16 fl. oz.	475 mL
4 cups or 1 quart	32 fl. oz.	1 L
1 gallon	128 fl. oz.	4 L

OVEN TEMPERATURES

FAHRENHEIT (F)	CELSIUS (C) (APPROXIMATE)
250°	120°
300°	150°
325°	165°
350°	180°
375°	190°
400°	200°
425°	220°
450°	230°

VOLUME EQUIVALENTS (DRY)

STANDARD	METRIC (APPROXIMATE)
⅛ teaspoon	0.5 mL
¼ teaspoon	1 mL
½ teaspoon	2 mL
¾ teaspoon	4 mL
1 teaspoon	5 mL
1 tablespoon	15 mL
¼ cup	59 mL
⅓ cup	79 mL
½ cup	118 mL
⅔ cup	156 mL
¾ cup	177 mL
1 cup	235 mL
2 cups or 1 pint	475 mL
3 cups	700 mL
4 cups or 1 quart	1 L

WEIGHT EQUIVALENTS

STANDARD	METRIC (APPROXIMATE)
½ ounce	15 g
1 ounce	30 g
2 ounces	60 g
4 ounces	115 g
8 ounces	225 g
12 ounces	340 g
16 ounces or 1 pound	455 g

THE DIRTY DOZEN™ AND THE CLEAN FIFTEEN™

A nonprofit environmental watchdog organization called Environmental Working Group (EWG) looks at data supplied by the U.S. Department of Agriculture (USDA) and the Food and Drug Administration (FDA) about pesticide residues. Each year it compiles a list of the best and worst pesticide loads found in commercial crops. You can use these lists to decide which fruits and vegetables to buy organic to minimize your exposure to pesticides and which produce is considered safe enough to buy conventionally. This does not mean they are pesticide-free, though, so wash these fruits and vegetables thoroughly.

DIRTY DOZEN

apples	pears
celery	potatoes
cherries	spinach
grapes	strawberries
nectarines	sweet bell peppers
peaches	tomatoes

Additionally, nearly three-quarters of hot pepper samples contained pesticide residues

CLEAN FIFTEEN

asparagus	kiwis
avocados	mangoes
broccoli	onions
cabbages	papayas
cantaloupes	pineapples
cauliflower	sweet corn
eggplants	sweet peas (frozen)
honeydew melons	

RECIPE INDEX

RECITE LABEL INDEX

INDEX

ACKNOWLEDGMENTS

Midway through the writing of this cookbook, my son, Will, said to me, "I might need to take some time off from eating when you finish this." To that end, I have to thank my children, Will and Paige, for lending their taste buds, tummies, and thoughts to all the recipes in this book. I couldn't have done it with you.

Writing a cookbook is an intense process that involves writing, rewriting, and more rewriting— not to mention recipe testing, retesting, and perfecting. And every writer absolutely needs an editor. A warm thank you to Gibran Graham, my first reader and informal editor as well as my taste tester. Your perspective and guidance always helps.

I should probably also thank the three of them—Will, Paige, and Gibran—for being so flexible with what we ate for dinner while I was writing the book. It takes some very special people to not bat an eye as I made many entrées and side dishes to be eaten in a single meal. Or served a half dozen desserts at once.

To Julia Bayly and Kimberley Moran, I owe a debt of gratitude for helping test these recipes and offering honest opinions about the results. Your help was so very much appreciated.

Thank you to my parents, Sue and Rick, and siblings, Zach and Haley, for lending your encouragement and support for this project and so many others. Thank you also for being my frequent tasters for so many years. You've helped shape how I cook—and my ability to cook for large groups without worry.

A warm thank you to all of my readers of Sarah's Cucina Bella for reading my blog posts, trying my recipes, and generally being wonderful fans.

As strange as it may be, I must also thank *New York Times* food writer Melissa Clark, a fellow graduate of Barnard College. It was your advice to a room full of women at a Barnard conference in 2005 that spurred me to embark on a career in food writing. I cannot express my gratitude enough.

And an extra special thank you to garlic, ginger, soy sauce, lemons, tomatoes, and kosher salt. Without you, this would be a much less flavorful cookbook.

And last, but certainly not least, thank you to Marthine Satris, Elizabeth Castoria, Vanessa Ta, and all of Callisto Media for selecting me for this book and ushering me through the process so seamlessly.

ABOUT THE AUTHOR

Sarah Walker Caron is an award-winning food columnist and writer whose work has appeared in *Fine Cooking*, *Bella* magazine, and *Yum for Kids*, as well as on BettyCrocker.com, *The TODAY Show* website, SheKnows.com, and more. She is co-author of *Grains as Mains: Modern Recipes Using Ancient Grains* and writes a monthly cooking column for *Bangor Metro* magazine. She was named the 2015 Maine local columnist of the year by the Maine Press Association. Her food blog, Sarah's Cucina Bella (www.sarahscucinabella.com), has been delighting readers with a unique blend of life and food writing since it was founded in 2005. She's a graduate of Barnard College and lives in Maine with her two kids.